3/09

D1103901

THE STAR & THE CITY

Press Pavilion

INAUGURAL EDITION
June 2006

Mac Tully

MAC TULLY
President and Publisher

Randy Waters

RANDY WATERS
Vice President, Production

THE STAR & THE CITY

Monroe Dodd

KANSAS CITY STAR BOOKS

Published by Kansas City Star Books
1729 Grand Boulevard
Kansas City, MO 64108

First Edition

ISBN 10: 1-933466-15-4
ISBN 13: 978-1-933466-15-6

Book designer: Jean Dodd
Assistant Editor: Les Weatherford

Dust jacket illustration: Aerial view of downtown
Kansas City, Mo.. 2006
Back dust jacket illustrations: Top, Star Press Pavilion; bottom:
aerial view of Kansas City, 2006, both by Aaron Leimkuehler,
Advertising Photo Department of The Kansas City Star.
i. Star newspaper carrier, Olathe, Kan., 1922.
ii-iii. Star Press Pavilion, photo by Jean Dodd
iv-v. 18th Street and Grand Avenue, about 1920

Printed in the United States of America
by Walsworth Publishing Co., Inc.
Marceline, Mo.

CONTENTS

William Rockhill Nelson, editor and owner of The Kansas City Star *until his death in 1915.*

INTRODUCTION

Kansas City has lived many lives — cowtown to the continent, miller and baker to the world, hothouse of jazz and railroad nerve center. Kansas Citians have built skyscrapers and warehouses, made greeting cards and pickup trucks, built pleasant neighborhoods and spread the city far and wide. Every day they make news across two states and seven counties and countless subdivisions.

For more than 125 years, *The Star*'s job has been to tell Kansas Citians what's going on in their town. Gathering news isn't easy, nor is preparing it for consumption, nor is delivering it to every corner of the metropolis. It's what a news organization does to stay in business, but for *The Star* it has also been a mission.

Through the years *The Star* has done more than make money. It has marched off on many a crusade for what it thinks is right. Sometimes it has been gloriously right, occasionally dead wrong. Along the way *The Star* has made enemies and lost subscribers.

Usually Kansas City has been forgiving. The partnership between *The Star* and Kansas City has held. After all, *The Star* is where Kansas City learns about itself.

In today's technology-driven world, readers demand to know more than ever. And the newspaper owes them more — more color in the paper and more clarity about the world. That's why *The Star* built a new press and packaging plant and placed it right in the heart of the city. That's why it redesigned the paper itself. In the new world of news, information moves at the speed of light. On the internet, deadlines happen every minute, 24 hours a day. That's why *The Star* is always updating **KansasCity.com**.

Much has changed since *The Star* published its first edition of four pages on a small flatbed press. News gatherer or news consumer, all of us have accumulated marvelous new toys since then. One thing has not changed since *The Star*'s first edition on Sept. 18, 1880: The newspaper and its city are in this thing together. This is our story.

Following page: Star *employees gathered for a 125th anniversary photo at 18th and Grand.*

THE STAR & THE CITY

About 1890, when The Star was 10 years old, these employees posed outside the Central Street entrance to The Star's building, then south of 8th Street between Wyandotte and Central.

1880 ~ 1915

BRIGHT AND GOSSIPY YOU ARE

I t was a match made a century and a quarter ago.

Two newspapermen from Indiana, despairing of the prospects in their hometown, scoured the country for a place to start over. Between them, they had just enough money, plenty of newspaper skills, ample ambition and immeasurable ego.

Kansas City — busy trading grain and livestock and land titles, and emerging from the recession of the 1870s — stood on the threshold of its greatest decade of growth. Eastern investors were searching for places to put their money and watch it grow, and they looked to the American West. Much of that money found its way to Kansas City. That's where the two men from Indiana went to begin their newspaper.

And that's how the match was made — *The Star* and the city.

On Saturday, Sept. 18, 1880, the first issue of *The Kansas City Evening Star* hit the streets. The newsy four-page sheet was the brainchild of Samuel E. Morss and William Rockhill Nelson, late of Fort Wayne, Indiana. Theirs was a new kind of paper for Kansas City, but the concept was hatched back in Fort Wayne. Morss and Nelson, who bought control of *The Fort Wayne Sentinel* in 1879, charted a course that one day would become *The Star*'s.

The Kansas City Evening Star.
VOL. 1., NO. 1.   SATURDAY, SEPTEMBER 18, 1880.   PRICE, TWO CENTS

In Fort Wayne, the two determined that local news was supreme. Politically, their paper would not be enslaved to a party platform, yet never neutral in a fight. They priced *The Sentinel* at 2 cents a copy, undercutting the competition. With Morss' and Nelson's leadership *The Sentinel* proved scrappy, indeed.

Yet the economic potential of Fort Wayne proved too dull for their liking, so the two looked for a new place to apply their newspaper formula. After studying the markets coast to coast, they chose Kansas City.

1880	
Population	
Kansas City, Mo.	55,785
Seven-county total	206,000
Average number of pages	4
Average circulation	4,000

Facing page: Bird's-eye view of Kansas City, late 1870s. The Star began at Fourth and Delaware streets.

Hoosiers

Nelson   *Morss*

In the 19th century newspaper people unabashedly played politics, and politicians openly dabbled in newspapers. Civil War memories remained fresh, so American passions often were expressed through party identification. Most American newspapers identified themselves with one party or the other.

The two men who started *The Kansas City Evening Star* had politics in their blood and on their minds. Nevertheless, they created a newspaper that was notably nonpartisan for its day.

One of the founders dominates *Star* lore and is featured prominently in its masthead. He is William Rockhill Nelson, who was born in 1841 to a prominent family in Fort Wayne, Indiana. His mother was Elizabeth Rockhill, daughter of a landowner and onetime Indiana legislator. His father was Isaac DeGroff Nelson, who moved to Indiana from New York, where he had held jobs ranging from postmaster to school commissioner to census-taker. A Democrat, the elder Nelson owned *The Fort Wayne Sentinel* from 1840 to 1842, converting it from pro-Whig to Democratic. Isaac Nelson also served in the Legislature, although much of his adult life he concentrated on farming and horticulture.

Son William Rockhill Nelson was incorrigible. Indeed, he later recalled how his "chief end in life ... was to break up whatever school I was attending." Isaac Nelson tried sending the boy to Notre Dame for taming by the strict fathers, but their discipline did not take, and they expelled him.

"I never enjoyed being bossed," Nelson said.

Back in Fort Wayne, he became a lawyer. Joining his maternal grandfather, he developed real estate. Shortly after the Civil War — in which Nelson did not serve — he and a partner dabbled in a Georgia cotton plantation. It failed, so he returned to Fort Wayne as a building, road and bridge contractor. He made money, but it soon was drained by debts that his cotton partner had accumulated, and that Nelson had co-signed. Along the way, Nelson acquired an interest in *The Sentinel*, his father's old paper, and he maintained that through the financial reverses.

In late 1878, the owner of *The Sentinel* was elected state treasurer . Early the next year he sold his interest to Nelson and to the paper's editor, Samuel E. Morss.

Like Nelson's father, Morss' was prominent in Fort Wayne, having been auditor, sheriff and mayor. Morss was 19 years old when he began his newspaper career at *The Fort Wayne Gazette* and eventually became editor of *The Sentinel*.

The Sentinel having long been Democratic in sentiment, Morss and Nelson stuck with that allegiance. Nevertheless, its new owners pronounced that "the day of the truculent party organ has passed" and promised to act independently.

They chopped the subscription price in half, to 25 cents a month, and the single-copy price to 2 cents, and then boasted that *The Sentinel* was "the cheapest paper in the world." By the end of 1879, they reported circulation at 4,400.

Both were impatient spirits, impatient especially about their hometown's business leaders, most of whom they thought "as a class too conservative." Once-lively Columbia Street, *The Sentinel* complained, was now controlled by "old fogies who are at least a quarter of a century behind the times." When Columbia Street businessmen objected, *The Sentinel* replied that the "fossils" should "rub their eyes, wake up and try to realize that the world moves."

"Had the people of Fort Wayne the enterprise and the spirit of Chicago or Kansas City," *The Sentinel* wrote on Oct. 2, 1879, "there would be 100,000 instead of 30,000 people here."

So Morss, 27, and Nelson, 39, began to look elsewhere. They asked salesmen, entertainment people and others whose business took them from one part of the country to another to rate other cities by growth prospects. They rejected two of their final three choices, Brooklyn and Seattle, and on Aug. 2, 1880, sold *The Sentinel* and headed west for Kansas City.

There were bigger, richer cities, but the two gambled that in Kansas City a business could start small and ride the town's growth into a prosperous future. Positioned in the middle of the continent, perched on the edge of an immense and barely tapped commercial territory to the south and west, Kansas City was a good town to bet on.

Taking the town by storm

In summer 1880, Nelson and Morss stepped off a train at Union Depot in the West Bottoms of Kansas City, Missouri, then claiming a population of about 55,000. The depot, only two years old, sat amid the smoke and smells of Kansas City's primary industries: railroading, hog and cattle trading, meatpacking and grain milling. Shortly, Nelson and Morss began organizing.

They arranged for offices and production space on the second floor of a building adjoining the Pacific House hotel, on the east side of Delaware Street south of Fourth Street. Their small headquarters was about a block from the City Market, placing them in the busiest part of town — home to retailers and wholesalers, food markets and hardware dealers, and entertainment spots of every stripe.

They hired reporters and printers and procured a flatbed press through loans

Union Depot, a passenger terminal opened in 1878 by several railroads, sat on Union Avenue in Kansas City's West Bottoms.

The Star's first home, 407-409 Delaware Street, next to the Pacific House Hotel. A central stairway led to the second floor, where the newspaper was produced.

from relatives and Indiana friends, and through the $3,000 they made from the sale of *The Sentinel*.

In 1880, Kansas City had two daily newspapers that appeared mornings. One was *The Kansas City Times*, established in the late 1860s as a Democratic Party ally and still showing traces of Confederate leanings. The other was *The Kansas City Daily Journal*, which traced its history through several names, all containing the word "Journal," to the 1850s. *The Journal*, founded and still directed by Union Army veteran Robert Van Horn, was decidedly on the side of the Grand Old Party. Like most American papers of the time, *The Times* and *The Journal* viewed the world through a partisan lens.

Nelson and Morss would enter the field in the afternoon. That pitted them against the mild-mannered and rather uninformative afternoon *Kansas City Mail*, weakest of the existing dailies.

From the outset, the two claimed at least three advantages in carving out a share of the Kansas City market:

● Their evening time of delivery, which they contended was preferred by most readers.

● The single-copy price, 2 cents for their *Evening Star* against a nickel a copy for each of the others. Nelson and Morss bought $100 worth of pennies — 10,000 pennies — so change could be made. Subscribers would get six editions a week, Monday through Saturday, for 10 cents.

● News — lots of it, reported close to home, in all varieties, well displayed and told from a point of view. It was to be concisely written. A city editor and staff of four reporters were assigned to carry this out.

As for *The Evening Star*'s politics, it often boasted that it would side with neither party, remaining independent — but never neutral.

Neither *The Times* nor *The Journal* lagged in reporting news, but typically each relegated the news of Kansas City, Independence, and of Wyandotte in Kansas to inside pages. Much local information was itemized in lists, one paragraph per item. In both morning papers, the front page was consumed by advertisements and by dispatches from Washington and overseas, only occasionally as close as the state capitals in Jefferson City and Topeka.

The Evening Star would make of its Page One a smorgasbord, and local fare dominated the menu.

The first copies came forth from the Delaware Street office at midday on Saturday, Sept. 18. *The Star* was a "folio," a single sheet printed on both sides and folded and thus only four pages, each 13 inches wide and 18 inches deep. The noon edition was followed by another edition at 3 p.m.

As that Saturday afternoon unfolded, *The Star* gave a running account of a big local hullabaloo, the opening of a rail siding and small depot that would serve what was then the far southern part of town. That area was called McGee's Addition,

"*The great feature of The Evening Star will be its local news....News will be furnished of fires before the smoke has cleared, murders, before the body of the victim is cold in death, and weddings before the happy bride can collect her senses or the groom put on his travelling-duster.*"

— *Star*, Sept. 20, 1880

THE STAR & THE CITY

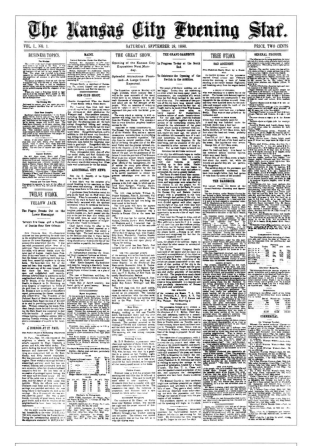

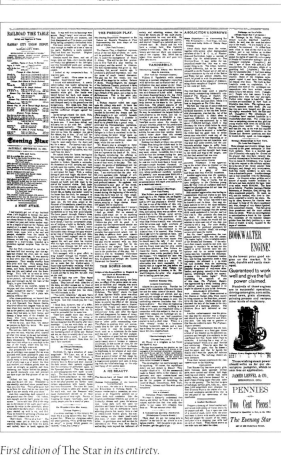

First edition of The Star *in its entirety.*

extending roughly from 12th Street to 20th Street for several blocks on either side of Grand Avenue. Its merchants had long dreamed of a connection to the railroad, so the opening of the spur was marked by a parade and by a barbecue — four beeves and 18 sheep! — for the public at Grand Avenue and 20th Street. *The Star* followed the parade in detail, breathlessly reporting how a team of horses had bolted along the route, trampling five children and killing a small dog. The midafternoon edition quoted speakers as telling how the new rail line promised prosperity. At 1 p.m., *The Star* reported, "the vast throng adjourned to dinner, after which the speaking was resumed, and is now in progress."

Volume 1, No. 1 of *The Kansas City Evening Star* numbered 6,000 copies, its proprietors crowed in the next issue, and that printing had been "entirely exhausted," newsboys pleading for more copies to sell on the streets. That was the good news. The bad, the paper acknowledged, was that a substantial number of the 3,000 subscribers they signed up received their copy late.

"In two or three days, at the latest, everything will be working smoothly about this office and *The Evening Star* will be served promptly," it said.

A couple days after *The Star*'s debut, Eugene Field, editor of the competing *Times*, had this to say of the new arrival:

Twinkle, twinkle, little Star,
Bright and gossipy you are;
We can daily hear you speak
For a paltry dime per week.

Field's greatest renown would come as a poet, and occasionally he wrote engaging verse for *The Kansas City Times*. Though the paper he edited was literate, it did not match the newly hatched *Star*'s "bright and gossipy" sprightliness.

That persona evidently was created by Morss, who ran the newsroom while Nelson tended to business matters. On the masthead, the two men were listed side by side, "W.R. Nelson, S.E. Morss, proprietors."

Morss, 27 years old when *The Evening Star* began, drove his small band of reporters to dig hard for news and to write it energetically and briefly and then go out and find more. *The Times* reported that he was in "high glee" over the success of *The Star*'s first issue. Morss also instilled a crusading spirit. *The Star* promptly showed itself a robust proponent of civic reforms, large and small.

Warming to that task only one week after its first issue, *The Star* called for someone to suppress the pandemonium that reigned on Union Avenue. With the arrival of each train at the depot, it said:

"Triangles are pounded, bells are rung, hotel runners shout the respective virtues of their houses and ticket brokers raise their melodious voices combining in a noise that is enough to distract the strongest nerved person. For the sake of the

A bumpy start

For setting up its small, hand-fed, flatbed press in its rented offices on Delaware Street, the proprietors of *The Kansas City Evening Star* wrote William M. Day a check for $7. Possibly they did not get their money's worth.

An unidentified problem — termed one of "the obstacles which are usually met with in issuing the first number of a newspaper" — delayed full delivery of *The Star*'s first issue until the Sunday morning after its Saturday afternoon publication date.

By the next Wednesday, *The Star* felt compelled to issue an apology for continued irregular and late service.

"The delay in issuing the paper is due to the fact that our machinery failed to work smoothly, necessitating use of presses situated some distance from our office. The carrier boys have thus been compelled to deliver *The Evening Star* after dark, at which time it was impossible for them to learn their routes.

"We beg the kind indulgence and patience of our patrons."

Once the mechanical problems were ironed out, human problems remained. A month into *The Star*'s existence, its circulation director made this front-page announcement:

"Subscribers ... not receiving their paper will please report. Through the unfaithfulness of one of our carriers, Lee Mitchell, a great deal of trouble has been caused. This lad is unreliable and unworthy of confidence."

reputation of the city, at least, some measures ought to be taken to suppress this intolerable nuisance that daily occurs there."

Three days later, the newspaper reported proudly that its article had set the denizens of Union Avenue at one another's throats.

"Last night they raised a row among themselves as to which of them made the noise complained of. Each one accused the other as being the particular one referred to by *The Evening Star*, until a bloody riot was imminent, and was only nipped in the bud by the interference of police."

As the weeks wore on in fall 1880, *The Star* would campaign against torn-up streets, sloppy streetcar service, political ineptitude and civic corruption in its newly adopted town. It wasn't alone. *The Times* and *The Journal* said many of the same things, but *The Star* said them stronger and more often.

Shortly, *The Star* aimed its crusading guns straight at one of Kansas City's most prominent businessmen, Kersey Coates. *The Star*'s complaint was over a theater Coates owned at 10th and Broadway — and a disaster that had not taken place.

"A Coming Tragedy," said *The Star*'s Page One headline on Nov. 9, 1880. "The Danger of Terrible Death to the Crowds Who Visit; Coates' Opera House, The Death Trap on The Hill."

At one set of well-attended performances, the article said, the crowd had taken 15 minutes to a half hour or more to depart from the second-floor auditorium, descend the stairs and leave through the theater's two narrow exits.

"Let a fire or panic start and what a terrible tragedy would result! In an instant, even a few people would block up the miserable, inadequate exits, or trample each other to death in the intricate corridors. The flash of a side scene, a puff of smoke or a scream would start a crowd to a terrible death."

Leaving no flaw unnoticed, *The Star* took the chance to berate the opera house for its fare:

"All this is bad enough, but a rat would forgive his destroyer if he but baited the trap well. In this death trap, the poorest kind of bait is used. With [one] exception...the entertainments are of the poorest character."

Coates — a former Pennsylvanian who acquired parcel after parcel of Kansas City land before the Civil War and who owned not only the opera house but also the Coates hotel near it at 10th and Broadway — was not to be trifled with. Two days later, he purchased space in *The Times* and spared no fury on what he called the "obscure and worthless little sheet called the *Evening Star*."

"Vile creatures have come into our midst, assuming the role of newspaper publishers, who, seeking our patronage, propose to coerce it by scurrility and abuse," he wrote of Morss and Nelson, the object of "these dirt slingers" to blackmail him into buying advertising.

"It will not accomplish the purpose. The Opera house will never advertise in so foul a sheet."

A COMING TRAGEDY.

The Danger of Terrible Death To The Crowds Who Visit

Coates's Opera House. The Death Trap On The Hill.

Kansas City is a metropolitan city in every sense of the word, with one or two exceptions, and one of these exceptions is its opera house. Situated away up on the hill, where it was placed in an abortive attempt to make Broadway a thorough-fare, it is inconvenient, old-fashioned, un-pleasant, and most of all, unsafe. THE EVENING STAR, ever watchful of the inter-ests of the people, desires to point out the danger to those frequenting the place.

During the Emma Abbott opera season, the old barn was filled for the first and last time during the year, and from the

Above: The Star's *opening blast. Below: Coates' reply* in The Times.

[Advertisement.]
The Opera House and the Blackmailers.

The above caption is suggested by a scurrilous and lying article which ap-peared on Tuesday in the columns of an obscure and worthless little sheet called the *Evening Star*. Were I not actuated by other motives than those growing out of apprehended danger to the interests sought to be damaged by this article, so stupidly base, I would not here invoke the attention of our citizens to the mat-ter. The fact, however, that vile crea-tures have come into our midst, assum-ing the role of newspaper publishers, who, seeking our patronage, propose to coerce it by scurrility and abuse, is one that the public ought to be apprised of, in order that such vampires may be shunned by all respectable men.

My information is reliable that such are the deliberately contemplated meth-ods for the accomplishment of their purpose. The article which induces this card was no surprise to me. I had ex-pected it for some time, having been no-tified that these dirt slingers intended opening their filthy budget upon the Op-

The competition

For a town of 55,000, Kansas City was well-heeled when it came to newspapers.

Oldest was *The Kansas City Journal*, founded in 1854 when Kansas Territory was established and when the City of Kansas, perched on the territory's border, felt its first big surge of immigrants and money. It was first named *The Enterprise*, and in its second year was bought by Robert Van Horn. In October 1857 its named was changed to *The Western Journal of Commerce*. Afterward, the paper survived several names, all containing the word *Journal*. Van Horn was one of the local civic luminaries, promoting Kansas City's fortunes through the columns of his paper and through his work in Congress. There, he had helped pave the way for construction of the railroad bridge across the Missouri at Kansas City, an event that pushed the city well ahead of upstream rival towns. A former officer in the Union Army, Van Horn kept his paper thoroughly in the Republican column.

Its opposite was *The Kansas City Times*, thoroughly Democratic under the leadership of an unreconstructed southerner and former Confederate soldier, Morrison Munford. Though he had a medical degree, Munford never practiced, preferring a life of newspapering and real-estate acquisition. *The Times* was established in 1868, and Munford and two partners took over in 1871. For a while *The Times* carried the banner of Jesse James, proclaiming his innocence and celebrating his Southern sympathies.

In an 1882 interview, *The Times* quoted a Jackson County lawyer as describing James this way:

"If he found a man that he had ever known so poor he could not put in his crop, his first inevitable act would be to put his hand into his pocket and give him the money he needed."

At the outlaw's death in 1882, *The Times* compared him to heroes of legend such as Rob Roy and Robin Hood.

The Times, *The Journal* and *The Star* were published within two

These three English-language dailies covered Kansas City when The Star *arrived.*

blocks of one another. Kansas City itself barely exceed 5 square miles, extending from the Missouri River as far south as 23rd Street and as far east as Woodland Avenue.

Third in readership was *The Mail*, which occupied the afternoon field entered by *The Evening Star*, although barely. Established in 1875, it had gone through an array of owners and editors in only five years, and in the late 1870s suffered a fire that destroyed its presses and stock.

The two morning newspapers gave *The Star* a kind send-off:

"One good feature about the bright *Evening Star* is that it won't have to do any whining for sympathy and support," said *The Times*. "It gives all the news for two cents, and this is the kind of a twilight twinkler the people want."

The Journal had this to say the next morning under the headline "Tea-Time Twinkler":

"Yesterday at noon the new afternoon paper made its appearance. As its name indicates, it is bright and beautiful and twinkles for the universe in general and Kansas City in particular."

Five years afterward, in a fit of anniversary conceit, *The Star* reprinted those early comments and placed next to them unprinted white space — representing how the same two papers had had nothing to say about *The Star*'s recently introduced new typeface.

Continuing the roguish comparison, *The Star* said that for the last five years it had been "standing on the toes of both papers."

"Tiresome as is such a proceeding, it is as nothing compared to 'stomping,' and that with *The Star* is to be the scheme in the future."

However arrogant that comment, *The Star* made good. It gained and held a substantial circulation lead on both papers — and on others introduced in the late 19th and early 20th centuries. Eventually, *The Times* would sell out to Nelson. *The Journal* would survive until 1942. Others came and went.

Nevertheless, once that season had ended, Coates shut down the house and ordered $45,000 in renovations. *Star* legend holds that Coates went to Nelson to admit that *The Star* had been right. Whatever happened between the two, the auditorium was moved to the first floor and other measures implemented to make the theater safer.

One partner bows out

In 1882, Morss abruptly sold his interest in *The Evening Star* to Nelson and left town. The reason was described as some kind of ill health. It went unremarked in the newspaper. In later years, Morss emerged as publisher of the *Indianapolis Sentinel*, and in the mid-1890s he was ambassador to France, appointed by Grover Cleveland. When Morss died in 1903, the *Indianapolis Sentinel*'s obituary said Morss had worn himself out in Kansas City and gone to Europe, where he underwent treatment from "an eminent specialist in Paris." Based on Nelson's life afterward, it is difficult to imagine the colonel's sharing power with anyone for long. To readers of the news pages, *The Evening Star* didn't miss a beat with Morss' departure. Nelson had learned well from him.

Now, Nelson was fully in charge, and the years to come would show he was up to the challenge. As owner and editor he never, ever, betrayed a lack of confidence. He would stay firmly in charge of *The Star* until he died.

Nelson was big in body, large in vision and grand in ego. His associates called him "Colonel."

"Not that he was ever a colonel of anything," one-time *Star* reporter William Allen White wrote decades later. "He was just coloneliferous."

The colonel-in-street-clothing was unfailingly ready to lead. Late 19th-century Kansas City gave him and his *Star* plenty of opportunity.

Among Nelson's previous careers was street contracting, and he joyed in spotting work undone or done poorly. Kansas City gave him ample targets. The city had leaped from infancy to adolescence immediately after the Civil War. Like many adolescents, it was still adjusting to its new dimensions. Among all its awkward parts, most evident to Kansas Citians were the streets. Most were paved only with dirt, alternately dust and mud with changes in weather.

A *Star* writer lampooned the problem in this poem, "The Wreck of the Omnibus," about a horse-drawn passenger coach that ran into a mess one day.

> *The mud waves beat on Delaware Street,*
> > *The inky heavens frown;*
> *There's a sullen roar on the curbstone shore*
> > *As the Omnibus goes down.*
> *With pallid lips the good folks say,*
> > *"God help the fatherless today!"*

> *Yes, help the dozen souls on board*
> > *And the captain on the seat;*
> *The grip-sacks wreck on the hurricane deck*
> > *Swallowed up in the pitiless street,*
> *With pallid lips the good folks pray*
> > *For the souls that went down in the mud today.*

The Journal and *The Times* had brought up the street problem long before Nelson and Morss arrived in Kansas City, and still complained about it. Yet, as was its habit, *The Star* kept the drumbeat going louder and longer. The campaign was a winner and typical of the paper's early days; a good way to win readers was to write about problems close to home. Everyone, rich or poor, had to travel Kansas City's streets. If *The Star* could claim to have slain dragons that endangered or inconvenienced readers, it could gain more readers and in so doing attract more advertisers. In the process, it helped those readers and thus the city.

Early in its existence, *The Evening Star* railed against the lack of progress improving Fifth Street, the prime route from the business district on the hill to Union Depot and the West Bottoms. The thoroughfare, the paper complained, was "a sea of mud in wet weather and for the same dreary expanse a desert of dust in dry weather. An indignant and outraged people, thousands of whom travel over this spot every day, raise their voices through the champion of the people, *The Evening Star*."

The immediate problem, it said, was a paving contractor named Camp, who had offered in February 1880 to pave Fifth Street with granite. After long delays, Camp found he couldn't get granite, so he offered to pave it with sandstone. After

The Junction, where Main and Delaware streets merged and were crossed by Ninth Street. Streetcars, carriages and pedestrians converged here. The view looks north along Main Street.

Nineteenth-century Kansas City

The boom times of the 1880s, which rocketed *The Kansas City Evening Star* on its way, came right after bust times of the 1870s. Eastern money, pent up for half a decade or more, flowed into the city. Big investors were looking for places to buy land, build structures and turn a quick buck. Their money was followed by contractors, and by workers and their families, all potential new readers. It was also followed by the hucksters, gamblers and liquor agents whose efforts gave Kansas City a seedy side to its reputation — and gave *The Star* much to crusade against. As landmark structures rose, so did political organizations among the poor and working class, sometimes helping their members, sometimes exploiting them, usually classified by *The Star* and other reformers as machines.

The city was a typical western town of the era, but it moved ahead of many others by the arrival of railroad tracks in 1869 over the first permanent bridge to cross the Missouri River. The railroad opened markets of the east, and brought livestock and grain into the stockyards, mills and bakeries of the West Bottoms.

That converted a town of only several thousand into a burgeoning metropolis. Business and population took off in the early 1870s, only to be brought back to earth by the national economic panic in the middle of that decade. Then came the superheated '80s.

Another recession would cool things off in the early 1890s, but not before Kansas City was well established. The city's central location, its position as railroad hub and its reliable work force drew warehousing and manufacturing companies.

By the beginning of the 20th century, pleasant residential neighborhoods were developing, as were parks and boulevards, and the city was gaining a national reputation. Part of that was caused by its spirited recovery from the Convention Hall fire of 1900 and from the flood of 1903. The 1900 census found a population of 163,000 in a municipal area of more than 25 square miles. Kansas City, Kansas, formed by the consolidation of several towns in 1886, added thousands more in population to that number.

more delay nothing had happened and now it was October and *The Star* knew his expenses were out of control:

"A simple calculation will show that a square yard of Medina stone will weigh about 800 pounds. Calculating twenty square yards to the carload and the freight at the small sum of $70 per car, it will cost just $280 per yard to get the stone from Medina, N.Y., to Kansas City. The cost of the stone, cutting the blocks, loading and unloading, laying in cement, etc., will be as much if not more, so that Deacon Camp will be out."

That was figured with the insight of a former road contractor, which Nelson was — and of a nascent press lord ready to lash out at the officials responsible.

"Break the contract," *The Star* said, threatening to hound city officials mercilessly over the Camp matter, "and repave the street, or the music will begin."

Hungry for more things to set right, *The Star* thumped for improved sidewalks and sewers, decent public buildings, better streetlights, and more fire and police protection. Looking back a quarter-century after its founding, *The Star* computed that it had donated more space to the city's streets than to any other subject.

Streetcars: the longest war

Any crusade requires a foe. Within six months of its founding, *The Star* identified one of its biggest and most enduring foes — the owners of the streetcar lines. *The Star* complained that the horse- and mule-drawn streetcar service was poor, the equipment shoddy and fares too high. *The Star*'s streetcar crusade would begin with skirmishes, move to battles and wind up in a siege that would outlast several streetcar ownerships and continue more than three decades, until Nelson took his last breath.

In the early 1880s, the Kansas City streetcar system was personified by Thomas Corrigan, onetime freighter, a railroad and construction contractor. He was physically imposing, and financially and politically powerful. In the 1870s with his brother, Bernard, he had started a horsecar line on the West Side. Soon Corrigan took over two more lines, leaving him in charge of all except one in the city. Among the Corrigan-controlled routes was the perpetually busy one that threaded the streets from the commercial heart of Kansas City down to Union Depot, the West Bottoms and the city of Wyandotte across the Kansas line.

The booming population of Kansas City moved most efficiently aboard the streetcars, even though it could move only at the pace of the horses or mules pulling them. The Corrigans found big profits from collecting all those new fares.

A young would-be competitor, Robert Gillham, had arrived in town in 1878 with ideas about building a new and better streetcar system. He foresaw a route ascending a special "inclined plane" on a beeline up the bluff that towered over the West Bottoms. Gillham's proposed route would carry passengers from Union

Depot due east up to Quality Hill and then to the business district along Ninth Street in far less time than it took Corrigan's horse cars to plod along the longer route that traveled northeast along Bluff Street to Fifth Street and then turned south.

Gillham mustered several financial backers, but his idea was sabotaged in the Common Council, the city's governing body. Corrigan, it appeared, had let it be known he did not want faster competition.

In March 1881, *The Star* joined the fray. It blasted the "street car influence" in city affairs and named names: "Boss Corrigan took snuff Wednesday night and the council promptly and unanimously sneezed."

The problem, as seen by *The Star*, lay with the shabby, inconvenient and uncomfortable streetcars then plying the thoroughfares. Still drawn by mules, the streetcars of the early 1880s traveled slowly, were cold in winter and hot in summer, and often drove right off their tracks into the dirt streets. Sometimes they derailed accidentally, and passengers were asked to help put them back on track. Sometimes they derailed on purpose; when two drivers met without a siding nearby, one simply drove off the track, into the street and around the other car.

The battle between *The Star* and Corrigan raged on year after year. *The Star* cried that the Corrigan interests had "taken Kansas City by the throat and, unless its grip is shaken, will choke it to death."

A group of St. Louis investors proposed to build an elevated rail line across the West Bottoms to Kansas, another threat to Corrigan's street-level horsecars. The council defeated that plan, eight to four. Distressed and disgusted, *The Star* wrote:

"Eight shameless men sat in the council chamber last night and openly proclaimed to the world they had sold themselves....

"Eight shameless men walk the streets today despised by their fellows and, unless we submit to the doctrine of total depravity, despising themselves."

Having beaten back his competitors, Corrigan asked the council to extend his own franchise 30 years. White-hot with fury, *The Star* howled about "the daily outrages perpetrated upon the traveling public by Corrigan in the form of filthy, overloaded cars, insolent employees, jaded, inferior stock, short hours for running and long hours between trips."

Again the same eight council members voted for the franchise. Again *The Star* branded them "The Shameless Eight" and printed their names in bold type. A public "indignation meeting" was organized, promoted by *The Star*, which headlined, "The People to Rise in Their Might ...and Express Their Opinion of the Rascals Who Perpetrated the High Handed Outrage."

Feeling the heat and probably fearing for his safety, the mayor vetoed Corrigan's franchise. The council, clearly feeling just as fearful, upheld his veto and then voted to authorize the competitors' elevated road. For the first time, Corrigan was beaten. Within two years, he would sell his streetcar interests.

The Star cried that the Corrigan interests had "taken Kansas City by the throat and, unless its grip is shaken, will choke it to death."

Thomas Corrigan in a newspaper sketch.

Gillham in the meantime altered his plans and now proposed installing cable cars. They would use the new technology originated in San Francisco, where streetcars were propelled by wire-rope cable that traveled in a conduit beneath the tracks. With Corrigan in check, Gillham's cable railway was approved and began operation in 1885, traveling a steep rail bridge that ascended from the bottoms at the depot directly up the bluff to Ninth Street.

As Kansas City grew, so did *The Star*. The center of commerce continually moved south, first up the hills overlooking the Missouri River bluffs, then down the slope toward OK Creek.

Not six months after its first issue, *The Star* was reporting an average circulation of more than 4,000 and found it had outgrown its first home on Delaware. In March 1881 the paper moved around the corner to 14 W. Fifth St. By September, circulation topped 8,000. In January 1882, *The Star* purchased its afternoon competitor, the ailing *Kansas City Mail*, and renamed itself briefly *The Star-Mail*. Envying The Mail's bigger quarters at 115 W. Sixth St., *The Star* moved into them. The early moves were made possible by borrowing, first from old friends in Fort Wayne, later from lenders in Kansas City.

Getting used to *The Star*

Readers became accustomed to *The Evening Star*'s methods. When the newspaper found a problem that human beings created — and that human beings could fix — it came out swinging. Through the years the paper complained about the quality and then the cost of natural gas. It railed against bad butter and short-weighted bread, and the quality and capacity of the city water plant, which drew from the already polluted Kansas River.

 In cases like those of Coates and his opera house, or Camp and his paving contract, or Corrigan and his streetcars, a single individual faced *The Star*'s broadsides, usually by name. In other cases, government as a body might be blamed. And sometimes Kansas Citians might be their own problem, through lack of vision or imagination or initiative. In any case, *The Star* invariably called for change on behalf of "the people." It was "the people" who wanted lower gas rates, and "the people" who demanded better streetcar service.

Eventually pavement was laid on street after street and Kansas City became passable in all weathers. Now, *The Star* reasoned, the city could improve its looks, too. Streets could be transformed into wide boulevards lined with grass and trees and sidewalks. And the boulevards could lead to open spaces where the vast majority of Kansas Citians who had no open lawns or shady verandas could relax and play and breathe fresh air.

With a population of over 65,000 Kansas City has no public park, no place of resort where the people can congregate with their families and spend a

BY THE THROAT,

THE STREET RAILWAY MO-NOPOLY HAS THIS COM-MUNITY.

Mr. Corrigan's Net Work of Poorly Constructed and Badly Managed Narrow Guage Street Railways—His Possession of the Most Desirable Streets and Avenues in the City—His Fifth-st. Bonanza and What It Might Be Made to Yield the City—How He Has Fought Every Scheme to Afford Suitable Access to the Bottoms—Instances of the Servility of the Council, and the Pliability of a Mayor—Length of Time His Franchises Have to Run—Some of the Ways in Which the One Man Power is Exercised in Kansas City—Important Facts for the Consideration of Tax Payers,

The street railway franchises which have been granted from time to time by the council, as recited in the last two issues, have been absorbed, consolidated and purchased within the past six or seven years until they are all held (with the exception of the Westport line) by com-

pleasant hour or so, away from the hot and dusty streets.

— Editorial in *The Star*, May 19, 1881

Thus *The Star* began perhaps its proudest crusade, the push for parks in Kansas City. Every Sunday afternoon, the editorial continued, the need for a park was illustrated by the throngs gathered at the fairgrounds southeast of 12th and Campbell streets wandering "aimlessly about, the only attractions there being the green grass and shade trees." Soon, the fairgrounds would be sold. The city had missed opportunities to buy that land for a park.

"Is it not about time that the young metropolis of the border should be taking some steps to provide a public park?" *The Star* asked. "There will never be a more favorable opportunity than now."

That was the young paper's first foray into the issue. *The Journal* and *The Times* had already made noises on the subject, In 1880, *The Times* even announced that "the era of boulevard and park building has been fairly inaugurated." But *The Times* spoke too soon.

More than a decade passed before that era really began. In that time, *The Star* charged to the front. When Nelson wanted something — and he wanted a lot of things for Kansas City — he mustered all his editorial forces for the struggle.

Consistently, Nelson demanded an end to Kansas City's municipal ugliness, whether it was corruption in government, decaying buildings or poorly kept streets.

For one thing, he loved beauty. As his paper grew and his own financial status improved with it, Nelson bought a house and land on the north side of Brush Creek and continually added to it. The house became a rambling mansion with walls largely of native limestone. He called it Oak Hall. Limestone fences bordered his own land. Nelson developed properties around it, named the area the Rockhill District and continued the limestone

Nelson's Oak Hall atop a gentle slope north of Brush Creek. Many rooms and much limestone would be added to it over the years.

walls along adjoining streets. He built a limestone arched bridge over Brush Creek.

For another, Nelson saw boulevard-building as an extension of his push for better thoroughfares.

In the 1880s *The Star* became the chief publicity agent of the parks campaign, and Nelson himself stood among its leaders. *The Star* reprinted articles from newspapers in other cities that already had fine parks systems — chief among them Chicago. It ran editorials. And it ran lengthy news articles that differed little

This was the dream. Development of Kansas City's boulevards would create the Sunken Gardens where the Paseo was crossed by 12th Street.

from the editorials. The drumbeat was on once again, and Kansas Citians could not avoid it.

Yet a mess of legal roadblocks lay along this road. Laws had to be changed and the lawsuits overcome.

Since 1875, Kansas City had been empowered to condemn land for public use. However, the city was required to pay the full price for it before taking possession. It could issue bonds, but not without permission from the Missouri General Assembly. Additionally, parks advocates feared that direct city control over parks would leave them open to raw political manipulation.

The parks movement proposed, and voters approved, a charter amendment establishing a separate parks board., yet the amendment did not give the board power to issue bonds. In 1889 backers won from the General Assembly legislation to overcome the problem, but in 1891 the Missouri Supreme Court struck that down. Back the parks advocates went, asking voters for another charter amendment. So the struggle raged through ballot box and legislative chamber and courtroom until well past the beginning of the 20th century.

None of that deterred Nelson and his *Star*.

Nor did it deter other Kansas Citians such as August Meyer, multimillionaire owner of a Kansas-side mineral smelting plant and an ardent advocate of beautification. Meyer, whose home lay a stone's throw from Nelson's, was selected to lead a new park board authorized by a city charter amendment in 1892. The board hired George Kessler, who had come to Kansas City to plan parks for a railroad line and stayed to develop neighborhoods. He drew up the new parks board's first comprehensive plan. It was issued in October 1893 and argued that attractive scenery placed intelligently would draw not only visitors but also investment and civic pride.

The first plan called for three major parks. One would consume the West Bluffs, an eyesore of tumbledown shacks and billboards that greeted travelers arriving at Union Depot. Another would cover the North Bluffs overlooking the Missouri River and the third the Penn Street ravine. Boulevards would connect the latter two and there would also be lesser parks.

In 1895, after a vigorous campaign by businessmen, lawyers, politicians of all stripes and *The Star*, amendments to the city charter were overwhelmingly approved giving the parks board the power it needed to begin work. A year later, the Missouri Supreme Court upheld the effort.

Now the parks foes turned to delaying construction, hoping that news of higher tax assessments would stir up opposition among property owners.

In June 1896, wealthy landowner Thomas Swope contributed more than 1,300 acres southeast of the city for use as a park. Yet Swope owned property closer inside the city limits, too. If parks were to be built near that property, he feared his tax assessments would rise. *The Star* had hailed Swope's donation of his vast acreage, but it condemned him and other foes in the newly organized Taxpayers League as "mossbacks." These people, *The Star* complained, had made money selling their land as Kansas City spread outward. Too rarely, it said, did they improve their properties themselves, or even tend them. For their part, the Taxpayers League complained about the potential tax burden and about the possibility their property might be condemned for a park.

As *The Star* recounted the struggle, "the proposal to provide lawns and woods and meadows and playgrounds and flower gardens for the people met no approval from these gentlemen, amply endowed as they were with woods and meadows of their own."

The "mossbacks" fought back in court. As always Nelson and his newspaper relished a fight.

Lampooning them in spring 1897, *The Star* placed on its front page a cartoon showing Swope (labeled "Colonel Stope") addressing fellow parks opponents. "Stope" stood on a small raft floating in a shallow pool in a debris-ridden lot

Greasing palms

Decades after Nelson's death, *The Star* reported that the colonel had once confided to his associates how the campaign for parks had cost more than newsprint and ink.

Hugh McGowan, a local political leader with a strong following and a friend of Nelson's, called on him one day.

"Colonel," he said, "you seem to feel strongly about this amendment."

"It's the biggest thing that has been before Kansas City in years," Nelson replied.

"Well, if you want it you can have it. But it will take a little money for the workers."

Practicality overcoming ethics, *The Star* said, "the details were arranged, and the votes were forthcoming."

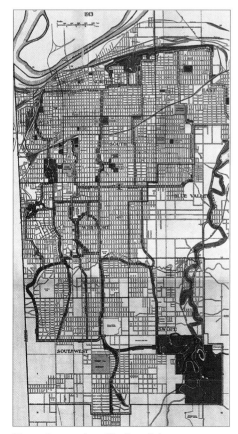

Kansas City's parks and boulevard plan nearing its full flowering, 1913.

Nelson the volcano

"A big, laughing, fat, good-natured, rollicking, haw-hawing person," wrote William Allen White of his onetime boss and longtime friend, William Rockhill Nelson. He "loved a drink, a steak, a story, and a fight — strong men shuddered and turned away from the spectacle."

Of all the larger-than-life people Kansas City has produced, Nelson surely ranks near the top.

"He had a massive dignity that large men sometimes have," White recalled, referring of course to the colonel's waist, and neck, and manner, too. He was a "hulking, jovial, irrepressible soul, moving like a cumulus cloud through its earthly habitat."

Julian Street, a reporter for *Collier's* magazine, declared that Nelson's power "was perhaps greater than that of any other single newspaper publisher in the country." Kansas City was fortunate, he said, that the power had been exercised by such a "pure idealist."

After his interview with the colonel, Street described Nelson as a volcano.

"He is more like one than any other man I have ever met. He is even shaped like one, being mountainous in his proportions and also in the way he tapers upward from his vast waist to his snow-capped 'peak.' Even the voice which proceeds from the Colonel's 'crater' is Vesuvian: hoarse, deep, rumbling, strong.

"The Colonel's enemies have tried, on various occasions, to 'get' him, but without distinguished success," Street wrote. "The Colonel goes into a fight with joy."

Nelson, the self-proclaimed "bad boy" of his youth whom Notre Dame had tossed out, turned his energies to better causes than mere rebellion. Indeed, when Notre Dame eventually conferred an honorary doctor of laws degree on Nelson, he wrote the college, apologizing for being unable to attend the ceremony and recalling how he had been kicked out of school.

"Had I been able to be present," Nelson wrote, "I should perhaps have ventured to say a word in behalf of the bad boy as exemplified in my own case.

"It was my disposition to feel that no one had any rights over me. Notre Dame, however, did the best it could with such unpromising material, and I have always looked back on it with regard and affection."

Perhaps, he ended, his story would "afford encouragement to mischievous boys and make them feel that their case is not altogether hopeless."

"His employees," wrote Oswald Garrison Villard in *The Nation*, "readily caught his spirit and reflected it clearly. *The Star* succeeded precisely as it embodied the qualities of its owner, including his rugged honesty, and precisely as Mr. Nelson would have succeeded in anything he went into by reason of his homely, forceful character and the sheer weight of his personality."

Employees also caught that Nelson was the boss.

"He would ask for something only once," ex-*Star* reporter Courtney Rylie Cooper recalled in *The Saturday Evening Post*. "then he bellowed.

"I believe he got a certain amount of humor out of the fearful respect which his presence engendered," Cooper continued, recalling his days in the building at 11th Street and Grand Avenue. "At odd times he would come slowly down the long, dark hall from his office and, with head raised, sweep a pivotlike glance over the city room. Instantly, reporters bent feverishly to their work. He would turn slowly and trundle back to this office without a word, but with a pensive twinkle in his eyes."

Cooper's time at *The Star* ended in a cataclysm. He was writing fiction in his off-hours — and being paid for it — when Nelson summoned him to his desk in the big newsroom of the new building at 18th Street and Grand Avenue, and said:

"You understand that if you have a good story in your system, *The Star* wants it?"

Over Cooper's protests that his freelance work was fiction, Nelson replied, "Fiction or

not, your first duty is to *The Star*."

Cooper defied Nelson to his face — and was fired. Eventually, Cooper made his way to New York City and applied for work at the *New York World*. Told he'd need a recommendation, Cooper wrote Nelson, doubting he'd hear anything. Instead, he found in his mailbox a week later a recommendation "at the highest possible notch" signed by William Rockhill Nelson of *The Kansas City Star*.

Above: Nelson dines while vacationing in the mountains. Right: Nelson in his prime — sole owner of The Star *and self-designated mentor for Kansas City. Facing page: Full portrait made in Rome.*

Onward into battle!

"*The Star* never loses," William Rockhill Nelson said. But of course it did, and frequently enough to give hope and comfort to those who opposed it. What Nelson meant was that no single battle, no one election or lone court case, should stop it on its many crusades.

Once, chivalric tongue planted firmly in cheek, the paper acknowledged this about its many quests: "And while there are Plumes and Spurs and captured Banners, there are shattered Lances as well, and broken Swords."

So for every grand victory over "franchise-grabbers," or "hammer-and-padlock" club members, there were losses. Even while Nelson was still alive, *The Star* acknowledged these failures:

● A $2.50 poll tax, refundable upon casting a ballot, aimed at compelling every eligible Kansas Citian to vote.

● Removal of telephone poles from the streets.

● Dispensing justice free to everyone, much like small-claims courts and legal aid, only applied to all levels of justice and universally. No longer would lawyers have been hired by plaintiffs or defendants. They would have been like police, paid through government and their services available to anyone.

● A Kansas City-to-St. Louis riverboat line, intended to help Kansas City shippers avoid high railroad freight charges.

Some crusades were extremely idealistic. A firm believer in free public baths as a way to a happier, healthier public, Nelson arranged to stage a show at Convention Hall to raise money for them. He paid for hall rental, music, decorations and printing. So on the Monday night after Easter in early April 1899, before a packed audience at the brand-new Convention Hall, the show got under way. First came a rendition of *The Kansas City Star March*, by Allesandro Liberati, the composer. Then the master of ceremonies proclaimed, "Let the Bug Hop!" As a line of performers began to dance, a 120-voice chorus roared into a medley of popular songs.

One soloist sang :

"So, whenever you're in doubt, go take a bath.
It will cool your burning brow and calm your wrath.
There's no excuse, you see, Colonel Nelson's made them free,
So-o-o-o, whenever you're in doubt go take a bath."

There were great causes, like upgrading the city water supply. Early in its existence, *The Star* complained about water drawn from the Kansas River, then the dumping ground for debris from the West Bottoms stockyards and packing houses. Discolored, sometimes foul-tasting and of uncertain pressure, the water was found thoroughly lacking. Eventually, a waterworks was built drawing water from the Missouri River, which *The Star* preferred greatly to "Eau de Kaw."

A favorite target was the natural gas provider United Gas Improvement Co., which had cranked prices up to $1.65 a thousand cubic feet and was seeking a renewal of its 30-year franchise. In 1894 *The Star* revealed a plan to renew the franchise at $1.40. Believing gas ought to cost no more than $1, the paper was outraged and went to war, with several city officials alongside. The "dollar gas" campaign succeeded.

And there were nuisance causes.

The Star crusaded against audience members who talked about the play during performances. At the opening of the theatrical season in 1903, the newspaper asked readers for their solutions. It was "deluged" for a week with poems, prose and pictures meant to make life hard for the "theater pest." Here's one reply, whose author concocted a script for a pest's interruption of Shakespeare's "Taming of the Shrew." The pest is named Tellum:

THE THEATER PEST IN ACTION"—HARRY WOOD'S ELOQUENT DRAWING WHICH HELPED TO AROUSE THE POPULACE.

Taking on the "theater pest."

(Enter in Audience TELLUM.)

TELLUM. He tames her — I have seen it all before (Takes a seat beside RESENTMENT and CONTEMPT, spectators.) She will make a good wife — I saw it all in the town of St. Louis a year ago. (Nudges RES.)

RES. "Twere best, though, wouldst not tell me afore, fear I enjoy the play less.

TELL. He tames her, being worst of the two. (Nudges CON.)

CON. Keep thy tongue, lest I tell the usher. (Swears.)

The campaign lasted a week, and afterward *The Star* boasted, "there was peace at the theaters nearly all of that season."

surrounded by billboards. Atop them sat "Stope's" audience, caricatured as an appreciative group of fellow landowners. "I am inspired to fresh courage by standing here in the last ditch which I bought for $150 a foot," the accompanying article quoted "Stope" as saying. "It is now worth $1,500 a foot."

"What use have I for parks? I have neither children to play under the trees nor carriages and horses to display on the boulevards and never will because carriages must be bought.

"Let us stand forever in one place like we have always stood and refuse to move one jot or tittle, one iota or one cent!"

For those it proclaimed mossbacks, *The Star* devised a Hammer and Padlock Club and had a newspaper artist draw up a suitable symbol. The hammer was for beating the life out of public improvements. The padlock was to "protect the pocketbook from invasion."

Eventually the Taxpayers' League tired of the struggle, losing time after time in court. By 1900 friends of the parks clearly had the upper hand and the system was under way.

From its early years, the parks and boulevard system did much to uplift the appearance and the spirits of a town built on railroading, milling and livestock trading. Although parks sometimes displaced poor neighborhoods — the boulevard and park along the West Bluffs were prime examples — they also appealed to the poor as a place to stretch out and to play. Certainly the boulevards appealed to the middle class and wealthy as places to build substantial homes and maintain property values. And the imposition of some order and beauty had widespread appeal. Kansas City's parks and boulevards would prove an unending source of civic pride well into the 20th century.

In its 25th anniversary edition in 1905, *The Star* boasted, "There are no enemies of parks in Kansas City today."

Bigger and bigger

As *The Star* waged its crusades, the city kept growing around it. In 1889, with Kansas City's population on the way past 130,000, Nelson built his own, classically influenced building on Wyandotte Street south of Eighth. Circulation grew by 33 percent the first year, to an average 40,000 copies a day. Like the city, the newspaper kept growing.

In 1891, Nelson launched *The Weekly Kansas City Star*, which circulated in

COLONEL STOPE'S EXHORTATION TO THE TAX KICKERS.

"WE MUST PUT A BOLD FRONT AGAINST THIS OUTRAGE—THIS CONFISCATION, THIS STUPENDOUS FOLLY OF PERSONS WHO DO NOTHING EXCEPT ERECT BUILDINGS, EMPLOY MEN AND WOMEN AND PAY OUT MONEY."

Swope

The family domain

Although his ego and much of his energy were bound up in his newspaper, William Rockhill Nelson lived an increasingly rich life outside it. In summer 1881, not long after he turned 40, Nelson began squiring Ida Houston around town. She had come to Kansas City visiting a friend, and Nelson knew the friend's family. She was from Champaign, Ill., where her father was a physician and had extensive land holdings. Before she returned, the two were engaged to be married. The wedding took place that November at her sister's home in Chicago.

Returning to Kansas City with no honeymoon, they moved into an apartment at 11th and Central streets. Their only daughter, Laura, was born while they lived there.

As Nelson's and The Star's fortunes increased, the three moved nearby to the Coates House. In summers they escaped to Colorado and frequently on weekends visited the resort of Sweet Springs in Saline County, Missouri.

In 1886, Nelson bought acreage on the north side of Brush Creek, then considered out in the country. On it sat a frame farmhouse, which he extended, and modified and added to time and again. The new Nelson home was named Oak Hall for the wood installed in its central room. Its exterior was native limestone, a material Nelson used often as his land holdings in the area increased and he constructed roads, fences and bridges. A horsedrawn carriage took him to and from the newspaper each day. Later he was driven in an

The yacht "Hoosier" required a crew of 22 for races. It was anchored within sight of Nelson's Magnolia, Mass., cottage.

Oak Hall after many expansions and remodelings.

The Baron of Brush Creek, third from right, with his wife, Ida Nelson, sixth from right and friends of their daughter, Laura Nelson. She stood next to her father, second from right.

automobile. His horses were quartered in a barn on the property, its second floor converted into a theater and dance floor used by Laura to entertain friends when she grew older.

The mansion, the property, the roads and bridges and the nearby holdings — all of this earned Nelson a nickname: "Baron of Brush Creek."

And there was more. As his wealth rose into the several millions of dollars, he began summering in Massachusetts, in the bayside town of Magnolia. Feeling a nautical itch, he commissioned the building of a schooner, which he named Hoosier and which he entered in races. It required a crew of 22. In 1907 Nelson built a "cottage" of his own. In reality it was a mansion with wide verandas, looking out over the cove where his boat lay at anchor.

Meanwhile, Nelson's manifold interests in improving everything around him led to a passion for improving breeds of cattle. He bought a farm south of Kansas City in the early 1900s, installed a water system, and built roads and a house. He bred shorthorns, some from stock acquired in England.

Over time, he hatched the idea of improving the common cattle

After Nelson's death, his effort to improve farmers' cattle continued at Sni-A-Bar Farm. Crowds gathered for demonstrations.

of the United States. For that purpose, he bought a 400-acre tract near Grain Valley in eastern Jackson County. He named it Sni-A-Bar Farm after the township in which it lay and a creek that ran through it. Here, too, he installed water and built a rambling house. Then, he set about breeding purebred sires to common cows, with the idea of upgrading the American breed — not only his own but also those of area farmers. It amounted to an agricultural crusade.

farms and country towns, saturating Kansas and Missouri and hitting Nebraska, Colorado and the Indian Territory — eventually to become Oklahoma. The weekly cost 25 cents a year, was filled with reprints from the daily *Star* and promoted the Kansas City marketplace and Nelson's political views.

Three years later, in April 1894, *The Star* grew from six editions a week to seven when Nelson launched the paper's first Sunday edition.

The Star's headquarters on Wyandotte sufficed only until 1894. In October that year it moved to a new building on the northeast corner of 11th Street and Grand Avenue, in the heart of Kansas City's thriving new commercial district.

Across Grand was Bullene, Moore and Emery's department store. One block west on 11th Street began a stretch called Petticoat Lane, lined with clothing stores and ending with the John Taylor Dry Goods Co.

With the explosion of retailing came a big growth in advertising, all helping pay *The Star*'s way. Further increases in circulation and revenue, however, prompted Nelson in 1908 to lay plans for yet another home, this on property he owned at 18th Street and Grand Avenue.

Walnut Street at 11th. The Bullene, Moore and Emery department store filled the northeast corner. Barely visible between the store and the building at right was The Star's home at 11th and Grand Avenue.

In the new building, Nelson decreed, there would be no private offices. Each floor would be an open expanse of desks, equipment and employees. Some said Nelson wanted to promote a democratic spirit; newsroom wags said he wanted to watch his help.

By the end of the 19th century *The Star* had become the dominant medium in the Kansas City metropolitan area, in western Missouri and across much of Kansas and the Great Plains.

Now, Nelson wanted to make it a truly national journal. Certainly, it gained a national reputation. As the colonel's fame and legend grew — his battles with the establishment, his unconventional tastes, his gargantuan appetite for food and for controversy — it became common for national magazines to publish interviews with him.

For much of his ownership of *The Star*, Nelson kept his paper nonpartisan, though he had been a Democrat when he arrived from Indiana. *The Star* backed Democrat Grover Cleveland in the 1880s and 1890s. In his later years, Nelson became a devoted backer of Republican and Bull-Mooser Theodore Roosevelt. Roosevelt became a personal friend and several times came to Kansas City to seek Nelson's advice.

In late 1901, Nelson bought *The Times*, long a partisan Democratic daily.

Several ownerships past its glory days of Eugene Field, the turn-of-the-century *Times* struggled to compete in the Kansas City marketplace. Nelson's primary aim in purchasing it was to acquire *The Times'* morning Associated Press wire service franchise, but in the process he transformed *The Star* into a two-edition-a-day publication. After he dabbled with various nameplates, he settled on "The Kansas City Times," above which a line declared it "(The Morning Kansas City Star)." Otherwise, *The Times* was made identical typographically to its afternoon sibling. Nelson called his revamped operation "the 24-hour *Star*." The two-newspaper plan continued almost nine decades.

Nelson considered *The Times* and *The Star* two editions of the same product. Each was to report news from the preceding 12 hours, and neither was to duplicate material printed in the other. Home-delivery subscribers, the vast majority of *Star* readers, had only two choices: Purchase twice-a-day-and-Sunday delivery or Sunday alone. They were not allowed to buy only the morning edition or only the afternoon. The cost: 10 cents a week by carrier, 15 cents a week by mail,

Likewise, some advertisers were required to purchase space in both the morning and afternoon editions. National advertisers booming the merits of one brand of automobile or soap were affected by this rule, as want-ad-buyers eventually were. Excepted were local advertisers.

Nelson, reacting to local brewers' opposition to his campaigns against saloons, banned all liquor advertising in 1908. Ads for patent medicines and clinical cures, a substantial portion of turn-of-the-century newspaper advertising, were screened from 1914 on.

Meanwhile, unwilling to pay high newsprint prices — particularly onerous now that the company was printing two papers a day — Nelson established his own mill in the East Bottoms in 1903. It lasted for eight years.

As competitors fell by the wayside, *The Star* expanded stride for stride with Kansas City, a city learning to overcome difficulties — even severe ones.

In 1900, only three months before the city was to be host for the 1900 Democratic National Convention, the nearly new Convention Hall burned down. Kansas City was stunned. It was a particular heartache to Nelson, whose *Star* had pushed to erect such a structure since 1893. That effort had required almost a quarter-million dollars in fundraising before the hall opened in February 1899. Now, it would have to be done over again.

And so it was. In the first flowering of what boosters called the "Kansas City Spirit," Kansas Citians mustered all the money and muscle they could and rebuilt it just in time for the convention to take place on schedule in July.

In 1903, the Kansas and the Missouri rivers spilled over their banks, flooding stockyards and packing houses all along the stream bottoms and knocking out utilities. Again the city rebounded. People started talking about a "Kansas City Spirit."

Always on the move

In the 19th century, newspapers often reported their own circulation totals to the public in their own pages, and at some papers the numbers were as much invention as fact.

Circulation numbers were the key to survival, not simply for the revenue from copies sold but also for the rates a paper could charge advertisers. The more readers, the merrier the cash box.

"Take care of readers first," Nelson has been quoted as saying, "for the advertiser will have to come if you do."

Based on its multiple moves and expansions, *The Star* was growing mightily, right alongside Kansas City. Less than six months after its founding, with its circulation exceeding 4,800, the paper outgrew its second-floor Delaware Street birthplace. It moved about half a block south and east, around the corner to 14 W. Fifth St., next door to the Western Union telegraph office.

The Star called its rapid growth "unparalleled in the history of western journalism" and characterized its press facilities as "utterly inadequate to the demands upon them." So it bought stereotyping machinery, from which a single metal plate could reproduce a page, and arranged with *The Times* for use of its presses. Evidently, the metal plates would be transported from *The Star*'s new home to *The Times* plant, now only one block away. Each page would be 2 inches longer than before, but the entire paper still contained only four pages. Twice more in 1881, the size of the pages was increased, and by September 1881 were almost one-third larger than they had been when the paper began. Circulation had doubled, *The Star* said, to more than 8,000.

The arrangement with *The Times* lasted no more than nine months. On Jan. 7, 1882, *The Star* announced that it had bought its

The Star's *second and third homes were at Fifth and Main streets, left, and Sixth between Main and Delaware streets, right.*

afternoon competitor *The Mail* and all of its equipment, and moved into *The Mail*'s old stand at 115 W. Sixth Street. It was called *The Evening Star-Mail*, a name that lasted only a month before becoming *The Evening Star*.

It found *The Mail*'s old presses inadequate, and had to keep them running from noon to 9 p.m. More presses would be ordered, it said.

The industry-advertiser group called the Audit Bureau of Circulation was not founded until 1914, so the accuracy of *The Star*'s figures can't be proved. But for those who wanted proof, there was this offer. On its second anniversary *The Star* said its subscription books and bills for newsprint would be submitted any time for general inspection. By 1883, it claimed 10,000 circulation.

When it turned five years old, *The Star*

showed off a new typeface and boasted of its new rotary press, a so-called perfecting model that printed both sides of paper simultaneously. By then, each page was 23 inches long, but the paper remained at four pages. Its conciseness and its afternoon delivery times remained marvels of convenience, the paper boasted.

The average American, *The Star* said, "is a busy, money-making individual" whose working hours "embrace the greater portion of the day."

"It is only in the evening that he can turn his attention to his daily paper."

A telephone line was installed, number 818.

In 1889, claiming a circulation of more than 30,000, Nelson built his first building

Employees posed at the Central Street entrance to The Star's *new building between Eighth and Ninth streets. The grander Wyandotte Street entrance, below right, led to a lobby and stairs, below left.*

strictly for the use of his newspaper. It stretched from Wyandotte to Central streets just south of Eighth Street. Advertising,

circulation and news would front Wyandotte, the pressroom and other mechanical departments Central. Now, *The Star* would grow to eight pages a day but because of a drop in paper cost the price remained the same as nine years before — 2 cents a day, 10 cents a week.

Within a year, circulation had grown to 40,000 and by 1892 to 50,000. Still a six-day-a-week newspaper when it took up residence

on Wyandotte, it added a weekly edition in 1890 and a Sunday paper in early 1894.

Cornetist Allesandro Liberati composed his Kansas City Star March *in the 1890s. It was played at Convention Hall, among other places.*
The hall, pride of the city when it opened, burned in April 1900 and was rebuilt in time for the Democratic National Convention to be held in it.

Skyscrapers were going up, the city limits were pushed farther and farther south, and by 1910 the population of Kansas City was on the way to 250,000.

Old animosities remained, however. The Metropolitan Transit Co. went before voters in 1914 seeking an extension of its franchise. Potential buyers of its bonds, the company said, were reluctant to invest unless the streetcar utility had a guaranteed future. Once again, *The Star* rode into battle, printing column after column of opposition coverage, and stirring the streetcar proponents to such wrath that they began their own small publication. Besides promoting their cause, it took out after Nelson. One cartoon depicted him as a spoiled infant, simply wanting his way in everything, all the time.

The nonpartisan ideal

Nelson was convinced the city needed to do away with party politics in municipal government, and he pushed for a nonpartisan commission governing body. Voters didn't agree, and in the process he antagonized some of the Democratic party leaders — or bosses. James Pendergast, founder of the Pendergast organization in Kansas City, had taken Nelson's side in favor of parks and of the new Union Station. Despite that, Nelson didn't like the way most Kansas City politicians operated, and he wound up supporting Republicans more frequently than Democrats. Even if he chose GOP candidates simply because they agreed with him, in doing so he was testing his own ideal of nonpartisanship.

Given Nelson's immense ego, his continual complaints about municipal malfeasance, his constant and rather imperious issuing of new ideas and the fact he owned a powerful communication tool, it is understandable that some Kansas Citians did not put him on a pedestal. Count among them many Democrats. At midcentury, one of those drafted a letter to *The Star* referring in disgust to the colonel

The forgotten co-founder

In 1905, *The Star* marked its 25th anniversary with four celebratory pages about its history, its crusades and notable deeds. Nowhere in the voluminous text did the name of either founder appear. Dominating the middle of one page, however, was an engraving of William Rockhill Nelson, captioned as "Founder and Owner." That year Nelson was still alive and still closely involved with the paper's day-to-day operation, and his name rarely appeared in its pages. If you lived in Kansas City, you simply knew that the newspaper was The Daily W.R. Nelson. What you wouldn't know was that there had been another founding father.

In 1930, Nelson had been dead 15 years but his associates were still in charge. Their 50th anniversary edition of *The Star* mentioned in passing Nelson's "Fort Wayne partner, Samuel E. Morss." Just as quickly, it dismissed him:

"Morss retired after a year because of poor health. He never was a factor in *The Star*'s history."

Even today, a plaque placed at the entrance of *The Star* in 1965 mentions only Nelson as founder. The same is true of the paper's masthead on the editorial page.

Despite being forgotten at the newspaper he helped found in Kansas City, Morss went on to a full and occasionally notable career in his native Indiana. After the long hours he spent setting *The Star* into motion, he went to Europe in 1882 to improve his health. Returning to the United States in 1883, Morss joined the news staff of *The Chicago Times* in 1883 as a reporter and editorial writer.

In early 1888 he bought in interest in *The Indianapolis Sentinel*, soon acquiring most of the stock and becoming head of the company as well as editor-in-chief. Always a confirmed Democrat, Morss headed the Indiana delegation to the Democratic national convention in 1892 and was a delegate to the Democrats' 1900 convention in Kansas City. He backed Grover Cleveland, and was rewarded in 1893 by being named consul-general in Paris, where Morss remained four years.

He returned to *The Indianapolis Sentinel* in 1897 and continued to direct the paper in various crusades — all the while maintaining its political activity. Meanwhile, Morss' *Sentinel* pushed for a new city charter, fought crooked elections and advocated a park system. It argued strongly that the streetcar company pay the city more for its franchise on city streets.

From *Fort Wayne Sentinel* to *Kansas City Star* to *Indianapolis Sentinel*, the similarities were striking, and Morss was the common thread.

In October 1903, Morss was sitting in the window of his third-floor office at *The Sentinel* when, according to one witness, he lost his grip. The long fall to the ground outside fractured his skull and killed him. Afterward, his secretary said he had had difficulty with heights and frequent bouts of vertigo.

At Morss' funeral, a wreath of chrysanthemums was sent by *The Kansas City Star* and a group of roses from Mr. and Mrs. William Rockhill Nelson. Morss, as it turned out, had not been completely forgotten — and rightly so.

"By intelligent, almost incessant work," an Indiana colleague said after Morss' death, he "laid the foundation for the million-dollar property *The Star* is today."

as "pig-faced Bill Nelson." The letter, written by President Harry S. Truman, was never sent but demonstrated a strength of feeling in which Truman was hardly alone.

By 1915, *The Star* had grown in circulation to more than 200,000 and was worth an estimated $5 million. *The Kansas City Post*, founded in 1906 largely to oppose *The Star*, lagged behind, reporting 126,000. *The Journal* trailed them at about 77,000.

Two hundred twenty-one carriers distributed copies to apartments and households throughout the expanding metro area. *The Star* consumed 70 tons of paper a day.

That marked the apex of Nelson's stewardship. On April 13, 1915, a few months shy of *The Star*'s 35th anniversary, the 74-year-old Nelson died at Oak Hall. Estimates of his wealth ranged from $5 million to $10 million. Accolades poured in

Inside the newsroom at 11th and Grand, the newspaper's home from 1894 to 1911. The building was impressive on the outside but soon crowded within. Platemakers worked in less-than-benign conditions, bottom.

Bursting at the seams on Grand Avenue

Only five years after occupying its new plant on Wyandotte Street, *The Star* needed yet more space. Once again, Nelson ordered up a new building, this one on the northeast corner of 11th Street and Grand Avenue. The seven presses installed there quadrupled the capacity of the presses at Eighth and Wyandotte. In October 1894, *The Star* moved in.

Besides being home to Kansas City's largest newspaper, 11th and Grand often was the site of big gatherings. Crowds covered every inch of street and sidewalk and some climbed to the crosstrees of telephone poles to see and hear William Jennings Bryan campaign in 1896. A regiment of Kansas Citians bound for service in the Spanish-American War in 1899 received a flag from *The Star* as hundreds looked on.

Meanwhile, *The Star* kept getting bigger. Fewer than 200 employees in 1894 grew to more than 500 in 1908. To help his family meet ends, a young Harry S. Truman found work in the mailroom there at the turn of the century.

Also from 1894 to 1908, average circulation increased from about 55,000 to more than 140,000. Until 1889, *The Star* had not printed an edition larger than four pages, By 1908, seven quadruple presses were printing copies that were rarely as small as eight pages.

In 1908 *The Star* announced it had bought space for a new plant, farther south on Grand between 17th and 18th streets. Designed by Jarvis Hunt, who would also plan Kansas City's new Union Station, *The Star*'s headquarters would contain more than enough space for more employees and more printing and distribution facilities. The paper called it the largest individual newspaper plant in the world, and Nelson thought he had built enough space to take care of the paper's needs for years to come.

It was occupied in January 1911, when circulation was averaging 165,000. That building, soon extended and with annexes and new facilities on all sides, is where the company stayed into the 21st century.

Grand Avenue at 18th Street in 1909. These buildings on the northeast corner would be razed and their place taken by The Star's *new brick structure, occupied in 1911, below.*

The avengers

The slashing style used by *The Star* when the newspaper was on the attack earned it a virulent set of enemies.

One was Frederick G. Bonfils, a native of Troy in eastern Missouri who came to Kansas City in 1886 and promptly began scheming to part people from their money through fraudulent land sales.

By 1894, Bonfils was in Kansas City, Kansas, running a lottery that happily collected ticket-buyers' money but never made a big payout. Smaller payouts were made by the lottery's agents, who later complained that were never reimbursed. The scheme was exposed in *The Star*'s new Sunday edition on June 24, under the headline, "Fraud on a Big Scale." It described the Bonfils lotteries as "all run in the same offices by F. G. Bonfils, formerly a Kansas City real estate swinder." In December, Bonfils was arrested and fined, and he shut down operations.

Shortly afterward, he met Harry Tammen, who proposed that the two purchase a newspaper in Denver, *The Post*. Bonfils moved his family to Denver. *The Post* was a free-swinging paper with flamboyant typography — red headlines and daily front-page cartoons. The newspaper shocked the people of Denver, but also sold thousands of copies. Bonfils and Tammens were now press lords.

In 1909, Bonfils found a way to get back at his old Kansas City tormentor. He and Tammen bought the struggling, three-year-old *Kansas City Post*, which had the backing of streetcar investor J. Ogden Armour. Armour used the paper to launch counterattacks at *The Star*, which was opposing a new franchise for his company.

The Post headlined articles "Nelson's Men Fail to Start Car Strike; Not a Crew Quits: Conspiracy to Tip Up System" and "Star Scheme is Again Shown Up!" Beneath, the paper quoted a "prominent lawyer in the *Star* clique" as saying the strike instigated by agents of Nelson would be sure to create sentiment against the company and defeat the franchise ordinance. There was no strike, and as it happens the ordinance passed.

As in Denver, under Bonfils and Tammen *The Kansas City Post*'s headlines screamed in red ink. Seemingly disingenuously, Bonfils told *The Kansas City Journal*, "We have no enemies to punish or friends to reward."

from officeholders, publishers and the general public.

The mourning done, *Star* employees and many Kansas Citians wondered: What would become of *The Star*? Since Morss' departure in 1881, Nelson had thoroughly dominated the newspaper and left a massive imprint in the city it served.

In 1908, Nelson drew up a will that would designate certain of his associates on *The Star* as its trustees, continuing his work and the newspaper's. But that was before his arteries became racked by sclerosis, which evidently affected his feelings about the newspaper and himself. The colonel's second-in-command for business, general manager August F. Seested, told colleagues repeatedly that Nelson could not stand to think of *The Star* going on without him. However, Nelson could not devise a means to support his wife and daughter if *The Star* were simply shuttered.

In April 1914, he drew up a new will. It made his wife, Ida Nelson, and his daughter, Laura Nelson Kirkwood, trustees of most of his property — not only *The Star* but also residential holdings in the Rockill district surrounding Oak Hall and his Sni-A-Bar farm in eastern Jackson County. From the interest off his estate, they were to send monthly payments to Nelson's surviving sisters, and the widow and two daughters of his dead brother, DeGroff Nelson. The rest would be theirs.

After they died, Nelson's will stated, the trust was to be converted to a fund to purchase fine art — paintings, sculpture, tapestries, rare books — for Kansas City. He added this twist: The money should go only to works by artists dead at least 30

The first instance of William Rockhill Nelson's gift of art to his city was the Western Gallery of Art, established at the Kansas City Public Library. In it were copies of paintings and sculpture donated by the publisher. Many copies were produced in a studio in Florence, Italy.

years — not as a rejection of the work of contemporary artists, purportedly, but to remove the possibility that living artists would try to influence the purchasers.

The art, according to the will, was to remain "at all times in Kansas City, Mo., for public exhibition." Eventually, that would become the collection of the William Rockhill Nelson Gallery of Art, later renamed the Nelson-Atkins Museum.

As for *The Star*, it was to help pay for the effort by being put up for sale after the deaths of Nelson's wife and daughter. The proceeds would be invested in property within 100 miles of downtown Kansas City, or in bonds of local cities, school board or the two states. That day, however, remained well in the future.

Saluting the memory of their dead husband and father, Ida Nelson and Laura Kirkwood signed this front-page article on April 21, 1915:

"Whatever helped the city, *The Star* was for. Whatever hurt the city *The Star* was against."

The paper would remain that way, they said, upholding the "great purposes and high ideals" of Nelson — and under the active management of Nelson's associates. The future of *The Star* rested with Nelson's wife and daughter and even more so with his employees — who now were their employees. And once the two survivors were gone, with whom?

The Star's artists at work

By the early 1900s newspapers were printing photographs using the halftone process. Still in its infancy, the technology was none too attractive. Nelson refused to employ it for his newspaper, thinking it would make it ugly. Instead, he employed a corps of artists. Often, they traced over photographs and produced elegant illustrations like these. Monthly calendars ran on the front pages in 1909 and 1910, above. Right: Scenes from the flood of 1903.

Star advertisements

1891

1890

1914

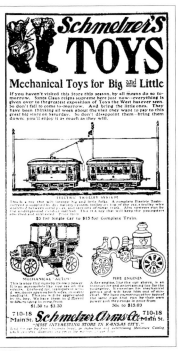

1907

1915 - 1947

TUMULT WITHOUT AND WITHIN

The president of the Kansas City Star Co. — cigar in left hand, suitcoat buttoned, right arm propped on a windowsill — wanted an update.

"Oh, Fritz," George Longan called to his city editor. "Anything hot in the local news today?"

Fritz Hinkle approached, bearing the answer Longan didn't want to hear:

"Nothing much. There's no big news in town."

Motioning toward the open window, Longan replied: "And there are a half-million people out there, working day and night, making news...."

That was on a fall day in 1929, when Longan had risen to the top job on *The Star*, and the Kansas City metropolitan area had passed 500,000 population. *The Star* and the city were roaring along with the high-flying 1920s, making money and making news most days.

This day looked like a slow one — until a reporter called:

"Hello, city editor? This is Moorhead at Police Headquarters. Stickup at 10th and Walnut. Copper shot."

"What? The hell you say! 10th and Walnut!"

It was a $50,000 holdup at a bank. A policeman had been gunned down, and the culprits matched the description of a gang of criminals then roaming the Midwest. The newsroom roared into action. Phones rang, commands were shouted, typewriters clattered, stories sent to press.

The scenario could have been real.

But on this autumn day it was an act, a skit performed by *Star* staffers in the second-floor newsroom and captured on the new talking-film technology by Fox Movietone News. It was made into an eight-minute movie for the entertainment of Missouri publishers and editors at their annual convention in November in Kansas City. The little piece would precede a feature film they'd see as their evening's entertainment.

1915

Population

Kansas City, Mo.	285,000
Seven-county total	551,000
Average number of pages	32*
Average circulation	200,000

* Times and Star total

In a scene from The Star's *talking film George Longan, right, asks City Editor Fritz Hinkle why there's not more news.*
Facing page: Police reporter William Moorhead phones in a big breaking story, advancing the movie's plot line.

Although the plot was scripted, it was scripted for a knowing audience — with insider jargon, topical references and sly humor. Any newspaper person would recognize the elements.

That was *The Kansas City Star* in 1929, showing its stuff. After all, the newspaper was doing a lot of things right.

Longan — his speech confident, his bearing regal throughout the film — had worked under William Rockhill Nelson. So had Editor Henry J. Haskell, who made a cameo appearance. Also in the movie was Roy A. Roberts, by then managing editor. Roberts had been Washington correspondent — *The Star*'s ambassador to the capital — when the colonel died.

By 1929, the newspaper's circulation was averaging more than 275,000 for the daily *Times* and *Star* and more than 300,000 on Sundays. Its seven-year-old radio station, WDAF, was one of the biggest in town and could be heard across the Midwest. The Star Co. employed more than 1,300 people. Indeed, *The Star* was big stuff. Surely, that was how the colonel would have wanted it.

Picking up the banner

By the time Nelson died in 1915, *The Star* was often ranked among the best papers in the United States. Theodore Roosevelt, out of office but clearly itching to return somehow, wrote essays that were published in *The Star* and distributed to other newspapers. It was his bully pulpit in exile.

The Star had always been Nelson's own pulpit, its course plotted by his opinions, his wishes and his whims. The colonel's lieutenants and foot soldiers expressed those opinions for him in print, carried out those wishes and responded to those whims. Under Nelson, they worked almost entirely anonymously. There were no staff bylines and no name on the masthead except the colonel's.

With Nelson's death, his wife and daughter owned *The Star*. Mostly they let Nelson's lieutenants put out the paper.

While the colonel was alive, Longan and others in the news department directed the writing and reporting, the editing and art work. They maintained the newspaper's reputation in the community and the country as a tenacious campaigner yet a lively gossip, clothed always in dignified dress. In journalism circles near and far, *The Star* was respected for its activism, its encouragement of good form and some experimental writing, and for its elegant appearance. In some political and social circles, it was despised for its presumption that it knew what was best for everyone. All of that continued after Nelson's death.

As for advertising and marketing — in those days the work of the "business" department — the paper remained in the hands of Nelson's longtime business confidant and helper, August F. Seested. Laura Nelson Kirkwood recalled her father as having no great talent for business. Seested, she said, handled all that. To Seested went credit for a multitude of *Star*-related events and gestures that in later

Seested

years would gain the name "marketing." Seested dreamed up an electric baseball scoreboard situated on the front lawn of the paper, loudspeakers to broadcast prize fights, free movies at Convention Hall and an election scoreboard placed there. Crowds gathered at these for big events, helping "brand" *The Star*. He originated a newsboys dinner in 1905, a gift to "*The Star*'s street merchants."

All the while, Seested kept a close eye on advertising rates and the books in general, adjusting here and tweaking there to maximize income.

The Star and its morning edition, *The Times*, passed through the 1910s alongside an enlarging metropolitan area, where the population grew by more than 25 percent from 1910 to 1920. Two hundred fifty carriers delivered the morning, afternoon and Sunday papers, fed by a score of motor trucks.

For more than a decade after Nelson's death in 1915, the newspaper continued under the auspices of his heirs and under the control of his longtime associates. To Kansas Citians, *The Star* acted pretty much the same as it had under Nelson. None of his successors, however, was quite like the colonel.

Nelson's power over *The Star* had been absolute. Ever since Samuel Morss departed, he had been the sole owner, without partners or investors or stockholders. His newspaper was the dominant medium in town and in the region. His monumental ego and creative mind — turned through much of his career toward making over the city around him — had found absolute expression in the pages of his newspaper.

Nelson arrived in Kansas City as it was beginning its growth into a metropolis. He claimed credit for some of that growth and some of its refinements. His successors inherited a full-grown newspaper in a full-grown city.

His widow showed none of Nelson's drive. Daughter Laura did, but stayed

Keeping track of each play and the position of runners in important games played by the Kansas City Blues, this scoreboard drew crowds to the lot in front of The Star *at 18th and McGee streets.*

On the day Nelson died, this illustration memorialized him in the center of the front page.

mostly out of the limelight. A few of Nelson's lieutenants had his ambition, too, but they would never own *The Star* outright.

Inevitably, *The Star*'s relationship with its readers and its city changed.

The editorial page gradually grew calmer in tone. *The Star* continued to argue its cases by claiming to speak for "the people," yet it changed some of its priorities. Never again, for example, did it mount a full frontal assault on the operators of the streetcar system. To be sure, after Nelson's death the streetcar lines rarely received gushing treatment, but the vehemence of the Nelson years disappeared.

Shortly before Nelson died, a count made at his request showed *The Star* had published 2,500 solid columns of type on that topic. That massive number and *The Star*'s abrupt change after his death suggest that Nelson had become obsessed with what he called the transit monopoly — no matter who ran it. On this subject, Nelson's was a fury that even his close associates could not sustain.

In many other respects his influence – like his portrait on a wall of the newsroom – still reigned at *The Star*. Kansas City felt it. Public officials would never feel the end of it.

Fighting for clean, efficient government had been one of the colonel's quests since the early 1880s, when the newspaper fired blasts at "The Shameless Eight." Since then, *The Star*'s forces had been sent to war time and again on behalf of clean elections and against skulduggery.

In the middle 1910s, the newspaper's primary official antagonist was Mayor Henry Lee Jost, who had come to power on the shoulders of the two major factions of the local Democratic party, the "goats" of Thomas J. Pendergast and the "rabbits" of Joseph Shannon. At Jost's first election in 1912, and for his re-election effort in 1914, the factional foes were trying to get along. In 1914, the year before he died, Nelson sponsored a "nonpartisan" ticket, which the colonel hoped would create a commission form of government. The commission form, popular among businessmen and Progressives in the early 1900s, typically featured fewer than 10 commissioners elected at large, each responsible for a certain realm of city affairs. The at-large portion of the idea was aimed at reducing squabbles over turf and interest groups.

Still working together, the Democratic factions carried Jost to an easy victory over Nelson's candidates. Months afterward, however, arguments broke out between the Shannon and the Pendergast factions. When Jost removed two Pendergast allies from important posts, ones from which patronage jobs were dispensed, the truce between the Democratic factions broke down. By July 1915, three months after Nelson's death, the dispute was so hot that it threatened to cripple city government.

A committee of Pendergast allies among the alderman demanded audits of all city departments. Those that refused were denied pay for any of their employees. Several allies of Shannon refused to be audited.

Roosevelt's friendship with Nelson, left, carried over to his successors. Irwin Kirkwood offered the ex-president a column in The Star.

Running with the Bull Moose

In June 1917 Irwin Kirkwood was aboard a train, heading west from New York, when he encountered Theodore Roosevelt, adventurer, ex-president and late-life friend and political ally of Kirkwood's father-in-law, William Rockhill Nelson. Roosevelt had plenty to get off his chest. That spring the United States had entered the Great War, but Roosevelt was convinced the country was ill-prepared to take part. He blamed that on the administration of Woodrow Wilson. No longer possessing the platform of the U.S. presidency, Roosevelt had only a column in a monthly magazine as his outlet.

Seeing an opportunity, Kirkwood offered Roosevelt a more immediate spot for his views in a daily newspaper, naturally *The Kansas City Star*. Considering that *The Star* covered the heart of the Midwest — and that Kirkwood offered him $25,000 — Roosevelt accepted. There was another reason for Roosevelt to relish a column in *The Star* — his close relationship and political bonds with Nelson.

The two met in September 1900, when Roosevelt passed through Kansas City after campaigning in Colorado and Kansas. That year, Roosevelt was the Republican candidate for vice president on William McKinley's ticket. Roosevelt visited Nelson on a Sunday afternoon at Oak Hall, and soon the two were friends. He called Nelson "a real editor of just the right kind of paper," and on another occasion wished him, "Good luck, oh staunchest of friends."

After the 1900 visit a *Star* editorial called Roosevelt "athletic and robust and intense at every point."

THE GHOST DANCE OF THE SHADOW HUNS

By THEODORE ROOSEVELT.

Ten days ago a ghost dance was held in St. Paul under the auspices of the Non-Partisan League, with Senator La Follette as the star performer. We have the authority of the German kaiser for the use of the word Hun in a descriptive sense, as representing the ideal to which he wished his soldiers in their actions to approximate. It is therefore fair to use the word descriptively as a substitute for the German in this war. It is also fair to use it descriptively of

Roosevelt's first regular column for The Star, *Oct. 1, 1917.*

When McKinley was assassinated in 1901, *The Star* praised the new president. Roosevelt responded, writing Nelson for advice. From then on, Nelson's newspaper focused on supporting Roosevelt's policies. In 1904, he carried Missouri, surprising in a traditionally Democratic state.

Disillusioned with Roosevelt's successor, William Howard Taft, and with the Republican Party that Taft led, Nelson followed Roosevelt into the new Progressive Party. He sent reporters through Missouri to develop the Progressive Party organization. Running the show was the managing editor, Ralph Stout. Gone was his nonpartisan, "independent but never neutral" ideal. One scholar counted the columns run by *The Star* and found Roosevelt had received 450 to Wilson's 66 and Taft's 40.

However, in Kansas City, as in Kansas and Missouri, Woodrow Wilson won. With the Republicans split, he carried the country. Roosevelt would never again hold office, but he would once again get a platform in his column for *The Star*.

Visiting the newspaper to prepare for his new effort in September 1917, he remarked, "The cub reporter will now begin work." Although *The Star* had set aside a desk for him, Roosevelt's columns typically were written from his home in New York or from whatever place he was visiting and sent to Kansas City by telegraph.

Beginning that fall with two columns a week, he later delivered them more frequently. The last was written Jan. 3, 1919. Three days later Roosevelt died.

WORKING ~~FOR~~ THE CITY

Kansas City officials on the take, as viewed by a Star *artist in this front-page cartoon of July 29, 1915.*

With indignation that would have made their late boss proud, *The Star*'s writers blasted away in a front-page editorial titled, "Collapsed."

"A row that started in a dispute over the division of spoils between two factions in the Democratic organization has now reached the point where city government has gone to pieces. From day to day nobody knows whether some important department may not have to shut down — whether the city may not be left for a time without water, without fire protection, without some other essential municipal services.....The public isn't interested in long statements from interested parties telling how it happened. It is enough for the people that it has happened and that their government has collapsed."

A day later, the audit committee showed the city was spending $3.5 million but bringing in only $3 million.

"Is it worth it?" the paper cried. "Do Kansas City's streets, for instance, look like those of a $3 million city? Do its mayor and council look to be of that value? Is it really worthwhile creating a deficit to get the kind of public service Kansas City is getting from gang government?"

Aiming to undermine the Shannon faction, the Pendergast-backed audit committee demonstrated where the money was going: to line the pockets of Shannon friends. One Shannon ally on the council owned a moving and storage company; records were discovered showing company drivers were paid for up to 15 days of work in a single week. For nearly a year, two city government clerks were paid each week for eight days and six hours of work.

On it went: water department employees used in election campaigns, a longtime employee fired and replaced by several workers friendly to the faction in power, applicants required to say they'd work at the polls on election day before they would be hired.

"Crooked politics," *The Star* said in a front-page editorial in 1916, "must work in the dark. Party organs can be controlled. They are glad to help crooked politics cover up. But independent newspapers let in the light. Light spoils the game. So crooked politics always fights independent newspapers."

The Jost administration's purchasing agent filed a libel suit against the paper, one of many it faced and usually rebuffed. The plaintiff must know, *The Star* said, that since the newspaper's inception "crooked politics has repeatedly tried to silence *The Star* by political libel suits. It must know that crooked politics never yet has succeeded. Crooked politics will not succeed now!"

The factional feud, detailed day in and day out in *The Star* and *The Times*, laid before the public how machine politics worked. As the decade rolled on, it worked in Pendergast's favor. His hired thugs appeared on election days, intimidating judges and clerks and ballot challengers and lots of registered voters. His operatives switched ballot boxes, replacing actual ones with boxes stuffed with illegal votes. In 1918, at a precinct where only 30 people voted before the end of the day, the

Pendergast candidate won, 700 votes to 1. The factional boss was gaining a grip on government — despite the fulminations of *The Star*.

Comics and magazines and radio and pictures

None of this daunted the city or *The Star*. Both kept growing. The 1910 census found a combined population of Kansas City, Missouri, and Kansas City, Kansas, of 330,000. By 1920, the cities alone had grown by more than 25 percent, to 420,000.

After the United States entered World War I in 1917, thousands of Kansans and Missourians shipped out for Europe and came back with big ideas. When the war ended, the city played host to regiment after regiment on parade, welcoming the doughboys home. A public subscription campaign begun in *The Kansas City Journal* and eagerly joined by *The Star* rounded up enough money to start building a memorial — the Liberty Memorial — to those who died in the conflict.

Star news staffers and ex-staffers of that era were guided by the newspaper's unwritten credo: Approach the news vigorously, and tell the story truly and well. Nelson had encouraged his staff to aim their efforts at the 30,000 "best people" in

Crowds lined Grand Avenue in 1919 for parade after parade of returning veterans, who marched beneath a triumphal arch. Usually, the troops were on their way to Camp Funston near Junction City for mustering out. As soon as the parade ended, they got back aboard their train.

An aspiring writer joins *The Star*

Eighteen years old and uninterested in college, Ernest Hemingway of Oak Park, Ill., had nothing in particular lined up for life after high school graduation. His father worried that he would be sent to war and wrote his brother, who lived in Kansas City. The brother, Tyler Hemingway, a Kansas City lumber company executive, was friends with a high-ranking editor, Henry J. Haskell, of *The Kansas City Star*. As a result, Tyler Hemingway's nephew got a job and *The Star* added to its roster a future Nobel prize winner.

The teenaged Hemingway arrived at Union Station in mid-October 1917, where he was met by

Hemingway in his high school yearbook.

his uncle and taken to the first of his local lodgings, a house on Warwick. At the newspaper, he covered police, General Hospital and Union Station. He followed strikes and watched excitement grow over U.S. entry into the war in Europe.

For some years, *The Star* had been widely ranked as one of America's best newspapers, encouraging its reporters to try their writing wings without paying them excessively. Hemingway came on board at $60 a month. By April 1918 he was gone, off to Italy to drive Red Cross ambulances in the closing months of World War I.

Ernest Hemingway never forgot his brief time at *The Star*, eventually crediting a junior editor on the city desk, C.G. Wellington, with channeling his verbose high school writing style into clearer, more economical English. Wellington himself had been on the paper only two years when Hemingway arrived, but he instilled in the young reporter the lessons of *Star* writing and grammatical style.

"On *The Star* you were forced to learn to write a simple declarative sentence," Hemingway said in 1958 in *The Paris Review*. "That's useful to anyone."

The Star copy style rules were crafted by former managing editor Thomas Johnson, and began with a directive that Hemingway evidently took to heart:

"Use short sentences. Use short first paragraphs. Use vigorous English. Be positive, not negative."

"Those were the best rules I ever learned for the business of writing," the author told a *Kansas City Times* reporter in 1940. "I've never forgotten them. No man with any talent, who feels and writes truly about the thing he is trying to say, can fail to write well if he abides by them."

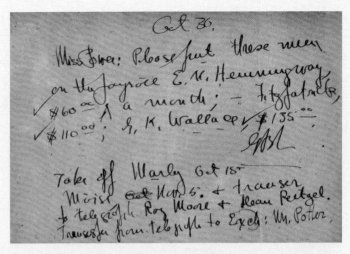

Handwritten on a small sheet of newsprint, City Editor George Longan instructed that E. M. Hemingway be placed on the payroll at $60 a month. Below: The style sheet Hemingway made famous. Bottom: A 1918 article attributed to him.

The Star Copy Style.

Use short sentences. Use short first paragraphs. Use vigorous English. Be positive, not negative.

The style of local communications is *To The Star*: in italics, out-of-town communications in this form. Salina, Kas.—*To The Star*:

Never use old slang. Such words as *stunt, cut out, got his goat, come across, sit up and take notice, put one over*, have no place after their use becomes common. Slang to be enjoyable must be fresh.

Use *Kas.*, not *Kan.* or *Kans.*, as an abbreviation for Kansas; use *Ok.*, not *Okla.*, for Oklahoma, *Col.*, not *Colo.*, for Colorado; *Cal.*, not *Calif.*, for California. Watch your sequence of tenses. "He said he knew the truth," not "He said he knew the truth." "The community

should like to see these abuses corrected."

Don't say "He *had* his leg cut off in an accident." He wouldn't have had it done for anything.

"He *suffered* a broken leg in a fall, not "*he broke his leg in a fall*." He didn't break the leg, the fall did. Say a leg, not his leg, because presumably the man has two legs.

"The work *began*," not the *work was begun*."

"He *was graduated* from Manual," not "*he graduated from Manual*."

Say Mary went shopping *with* Mabel —not "*in company with*" Mabel.

"Honor *the memory* of J V C Karnes" not "*honor* J. V. C. Karnes" after his death.

Say "John Jones of St. Louis," no comma between *Jones* and *of*.

"Mr Roosevelt is a leader who, we

others, C W Armour, J C N. The word *others* implies that t sons mentioned are apart from already mentioned, but the imp does not hold true. The sentence read: "Twenty attended, among C W Armour and J C Nichols.

He died of heart *disease*, nu failure—everybody dies of "hea ure."

Representative Bland, not *C mas Bland*. The members of h house and senate are *Congressma* titles "Representative" and "S distinguish them.

"He *suspected* the negro was not "He *suspicioned* the neg guilty." "The police were suspic him," not "The police consider *suspicious*." Do not use *suspec* noun.

The words donate and donati

MIX WAR, ART AND DANCING.

The Camp Community Service Gave First Party for Soldiers.

Outside a woman walked along the wet street—lamp lit sidewalk through the sleet and snow.

Inside in the Fine Arts Institute on the sixth floor of the Y. W. C. A. Building, 1020 McGee Street, a merry crowd of soldiers from Camp Funston and Fort Leavenworth fox trotted and one-stepped with girls from the Fine Arts School while a sober faced young man pounded out the latest Jazz music as he watched the moving figures. In a corner a private in the signal corps was discussing Whistler with a black haired girl who heartily agreed with him. The private had been a member of the art colony at Chicago before war was declared.

Three men from Funston were wandering arm in arm along the wall looking at the exhibition of paintings by Kansas City artists. The piano player stopped. The dancers clapped and cheered and he swung into the "Long, Long Trail Awinding." An infantry corporal, dancing with a swift moving girl in a red dress, bent his head close to hers and confided something about a girl in Chautauqua, Kas. In the corri-

ST. LOUISANS AWAY TO A FLYING START.

The Concordia Seminary quintet of St. Louis looked good in its upper bracket victory in the national amateur basket ball tournament in Convention hall yesterday. The Empire Oil and Gas Company team of Bartlesville, Ok., was juggernauted under a 19 to 47 score. The play of the St. Louis boys was brilliant all the way...

First news photograph published in The Star *appeared March 8, 1921. Small photos had appeared since 1915 in advertisements.*

Kansas City – the educated and tasteful ones, the schoolteachers and preachers who loved the newspaper's restrained appearance. Clearly, neither he nor his successors at *The Star* minded that an extra 170,000 and more also bought the paper, and perhaps those were influenced by something other than gentility. As always, *The Star*'s staid dress belied a newspaper full of everyday human-interest stories: the 43-year old pharmaceutical salesman who died of a heart attack on an Independence streetcar at Fairmount Junction, the police board's purchase of a stylish seven-passenger touring car for the use of board members, a shortage of castor oil in city hospitals.

And as always, the newspaper had its projects. One day in April 1917, *The Times* implored readers to "Finish 'The Scout' Fund!" — pleading in a front-page editorial for money to give Cyrus Dallin's statue of a Native American on horseback a permanent home in Kansas City. That afternoon, *The Star* reported that the money had been secured by a last-minute $1,000 contribution from Mrs. William Rockhill Nelson.

The economic boom of the 1920s rolled along for Kansas City and the money rolled in, both to *The Star* and the city. Kansas City was beginning to be reshaped by the automobile, which now much of the middle class could afford. New residential communities sprang up to the south, along with a shopping district based on easing the way for shoppers' automobiles, the Country Club Plaza. Civic boosters hoped for a population of 1 million by 1930.

The 1920s unleashed an age of advertising and marketing, which created a demand for new products, new methods and new technologies. This lined the

Taking to the air:
The Star's WDAF

The world of news and entertainment changed almost overnight in the early 1920s with the advent of radio. The first commercial station in the United States began in 1920 and within a few years, stations were everywhere.

Managers of *The Star* were quick to hop on board, obtaining a commercial license and beginning broadcasts over a 500-watt transmitter on June 5, 1922. Studios were built on the third floor of the building at 18th and Grand and were soundproofed. *The Star*'s WDAF was not the first commercially licensed station in the area, but it arrived within three months of the first. It certainly had the biggest marketing platform of the early stations — the two newspapers issued each day from the same building.

As radio buffs tuned in their crystal sets, programming began in mid-evening. Mostly listeners heard string music or solos and an occasional speech. Within its first year, *The Star*'s station came up with the idea of a remote broadcast from the Plantation Room of the Muehlebach Hotel, where the Coon-Sanders orchestra played. The program began at 11:45 p.m. and lasted until 1 a.m. six nights a week. Its title was "Nighthawk Frolic," and the band soon changed its name to the Coon-Sanders Kansas City Nighthawks. In radio's early days, there was little government regulation of signal power and little competition for frequencies, particularly late at night. The Nighthawks, then, were heard hundreds of miles away.

By November 1922, WDAF was broadcasting college football games from Lawrence, Kan., and Columbia, Mo. By 1925, the station carried regular network shows paid for by sponsors. By 1927, WDAF became a charter member of the NBC network.

Top: Star staffers described the 1932 Kansas-Oklahoma football game from the press box in Lawrence, Kan. Above: The WDAF studio. Left: Radio towers dominated The Star building until World War II. From 1937, the broadcasts, now at 5,000 watts, were sent from an antenna in Johnson County.

THE STAR & THE CITY

newspaper's coffers and also forced it to change.

Despite its competitors' heavy use of half-tone photographs as early as the 1910s, *The Star* had rejected using them. Nelson and his successors fretted that early half-tone reproduction was too poor. For several years, the newspaper employed photographers but did not publish their work. Prints were turned over to staff artists to be traced and turned into line drawings for publication. Occasionally advertisers demanded photos and by 1915, a few ads contained small photos.

In March 1921 *The Star* published its first news photo, a group portrait of a basketball team in the sports section. The door was open. Photos flooded the pages of the paper, and by summer 1922 a half-page photograph of San Francisco's convention hall dominated the front page — part of the newspaper's campaign for a new convention hall for Kansas City.

The newspaper also opened its pages to comic strips. The first strip with continuity — unlike syndicated gag panels and a humorous strip drawn by *The Star*'s Harry Wood, "The Intellectual Pup" — was "Mr. And Mrs." The strip, which featured the bickering Joseph and Violet Green and their son, Bertram, made its debut March 13, 1921. Sunday comics arrived on July 6, 1924.

At the insistence of Laura Nelson Kirkwood, *The Star* created a Sunday magazine, expensively produced. The magazine's cover typically showed a reproduction of some European masterwork, the kind of reproduction Nelson had purchased and donated to the public library's art gallery. The first Sunday of the magazine's existence, circulation shot up by 19,000.

Boldest of all the new advances was radio. In 1922, *The Star* joined the first wave of radio station owners in Kansas City, inaugurating WDAF. Studios were created in the building, and massive broadcast towers were built atop it. Another outlet was created for news, although radio in those days carried little of it.

The Star's vigorous growth and coverage earned it more than subscribers. It also gained enemies, some angry enough to try to run it out of business. J. Ogden Armour had subsidized *The Kansas City Post* in the early 1900s in an attempt to counter *The Star*'s attacks on his Metropolitan Street Railway Co. and Frederick Bonfils and his Denver pal Harry Tammen took over *The Post* in 1909, continuing the attacks on the paper.

The most prominent *Star* detractor of the 1920s was Walter S. Dickey, who had made a fortune in Kansas City manufacturing clay sewer pipe. As western cities grew and all cities improved infrastructure, Dickey's pipe was a basic requirement. The company grew to 26 plants in 12 states with branch offices across the country. Dickey also invested in banks, real estate and river barges, and on the side dabbled in politics.

Dickey lost a race for the U.S. Senate from Missouri in 1916 and in 1920, pressured by GOP friends, offered himself for Republican committeeman in Kansas City's 4th Ward. His opponent branded Dickey the candidate of the bosses.

Sunday special

Laura Nelson Kirkwood had dreamed of a colorful, elegant magazine to accompany The Star *on Sundays, and in 1924 she got her wish. On each cover was a reproduction of a painting. Inside were fiction and photographs, some of Kansas City society.*

The only child

While the Baron of Brush Creek was alive, many ranked him as the most important man in town. A legacy awaited his daughter after he died, yet surely she felt the weight of his fame long before. His letters to her, sometimes consoling and sometimes counseling, hinted that Laura Nelson commanded her father's love but not his time. Most days William Rockhill Nelson's work was consumed by his newspaper, or the people he wished to influence.

Laura Nelson was born to William R. and Ida Nelson in 1883, when *The Star* was just getting started and her parents were living in an apartment at 11th and Central streets. In 1894, when she was 11 years old, her parents took her to Paris, where she was put in school for two years. After a stint at the Barstow School in Kansas City, she was sent to Boston in 1898 for further schooling. Frequently, her father wrote her, scribbling notes in pencil on scratch paper. He counseled her on dealing with homesickness and on coping with gossip about her.

"The play of Scandal is brutal," he said, surely drawing from his own experience. "But it is good discipline."

In Kansas City, she loved having friends out to the house – the sprawling Oak Hall with its outlying barn, where a second floor was built for dancing and for staging plays, all overseen by Laura herself.

She became infatuated with an expatriate Baltimore *bon vivant*, Irwin Kirkwood, who had arrived in Kansas City in 1905 to deal in real estate. The two met at a hunt and polo club. Friends recall that he ran with a free-wheeling crowd. They recalled her as somewhat self-conscious — feelings that evaporated when she drank. She had to persuade her father to accept him as her husband, but eventually he relented and she married Kirkwood in New York in 1910.

Laura and pet, photographed in Kansas City in the middle 1880s.

After her father's death in 1915 and her mother's in 1921, she became the sole trustee of her father's estate – the person at the top of the pyramid of Kansas City's dominant newspaper. That year, she turned 38 years old. Under normal circumstances, *The Star* would have operated for decades under her

ownership – and her guidance through husband Irwin Kirkwood, named editor. It operated that way only five years.

Her wish that *The Star* publish a magazine devoted to art and literature, with a masterpiece reproduced on the cover each week, was based in her own upbringing.

"My father left all he had to promote interest in art in Kansas City and the Southwest," she said. "These cover pages will help educate people...to an understanding of the best there is in painting."

She enjoyed being part of the newspaper, joining in the conversations on Saturday nights at Oak Hall, where the top managers had traditionally repaired after getting the Sunday paper in order. As the person in charge, she wanted to uphold her father's journalistic principles, but she also knew the world of newspapers was changing. That would mean photographs, comics, radio — a gamut of possibilities her father either objected to or had never encountered.

Word in society was that she drank, eventually quite heavily. Over time, she appeared in public less and less.

In January 1926, the newspaper said, she had not been well but had "improved under treatment." In late February 1926 she embarked for New York to prepare for a voyage to Europe. Irwin was going to accompany her overseas, but their passage was not scheduled to take place until April. It is unclear how she was going to pass the intervening time.

The couple boarded a train at Union Station Feb. 21. Kirkwood accompanied her to Chicago, and then returned to Kansas City. She traveled on to New York and later that week headed south to Baltimore to see an eye specialist. There on Feb. 26 she dined with Kirkwood's brother, Thone Kirkwood, and his wife. They accompanied her to her hotel about 10 p.m.

Her maid saw her at 5 a.m. the next day, and later quoted her as saying she felt well. Three and one-half hours later, the maid returned and found her dead. *The Star* said the cause was apoplexy.

She had turned 43 only two weeks before.

Her body was returned to Kansas City by train, accompanied by Thone and John Kirkwood and by Roy Roberts, *The Star*'s Washington correspondent. Irwin Kirkwood met the train in Chicago.

Her funeral was held at a packed Oak Hall, where her minister spoke of her "eager spirit, despite human ills and frailty."

He quoted from a poem:

"Oh, the way sometimes is low,
And the waters dark and deep
And I stumble as I go...."

At Mount Washington cemetery, she was placed in the family chapel.

Executors promptly put *The Star* up for sale. Kirkwood and associates promptly terminated her Sunday magazine. It was hemorrhaging money.

Although Dickey was a Republican who had once been friendly to the paper, *The Star* opposed him. He lost the committeeman battle. The next morning, according to Dickey's family, he was stunned when *The Times* said he had "bellied up to the bar" after his defeat. Never a hard-drinking man, the accusation enraged Dickey, and he became obsessed. He spent much of the rest of his life trying to get even with *The Star*.

In 1921, he purchased *The Kansas City Journal* at a bankruptcy sale for a little more than $100,000. The next year, he bought *The Post* from Bonfils and Tammen, paying them more than $1 million. Until 1928, he published one in the morning, one in the afternoon and one on Sunday, the same schedule as *The Star* and *The Times*. In their columns Dickey's newspapers hammered *The Star*. His advertising sales force dropped rates to try to take business away. The effort would cost Dickey vast sums of money.

Dickey

Typically, *The Star* ignored attacks from other papers and it largely ignored these. More troubling, perhaps, were the rumbles it heard from within.

Last of the Nelsons

Profitable as the decade was for the paper, the city and the country, the early and middle 1920s were turbulent times for management of *The Star*, beginning with a small ripple.

In 1921, Nelson's widow, Ida Nelson, died. She had stood in her husband's shadow while he was alive, and in the six years since his death showed little inclination to emerge. Her passing was mourned by a three-paragraph front-page article and brief editorial in *The Star* — "a gentlewoman, kind, considerate, devoted to her home and her city, punctilious in all her responsibilities" — and that was that.

Ida Nelson's death left 38-year-old Laura Nelson Kirkwood the sole remaining direct relative of the founder. Something of an independent soul like her father, Laura dabbled in the newspaper, often pushing the men who ran it to pay some attention to the finer things such as art. Her representative was her husband, Irwin Kirkwood, who carried out her wishes at 18th and Grand and also began involving himself in the newsroom. After an apprenticeship under some of the colonel's editors, Kirkwood was named editor in the early 1920s.

The Kirkwoods acted as patrons of the newspaper and Nelson's crew of managers continued as it had. Kansas Citians — and particularly staffers of *The Star* — supposed that arrangement would hold for years to come. After all, Laura should have many years to live.

However, in February 1926 while on a trip to the East, Laura Nelson died. There had long been rumors that she drank heavily, but the cause of her early death was stated only as "apoplexy." Because she and Irwin Kirkwood had borne no

Irwin Kirkwood, leader of the employee-owner group and first president of the Kansas City Star Co.

offspring, her death ended 46 years of Nelson family ownership of *The Star*.

The event triggered the most important clause of Nelson's will: The newspaper must be sold. The proceeds were to be used to acquire art for the people of Kansas City. How many paintings and sculptures could be purchased and of what quality depended on one thing — how much *The Star* would draw on the market.

For the city, the benefit would be obvious. For the staff of *The Star*, however, the sale could be cataclysmic. Who would buy it? How would they run it? Which employees would they keep and which policies would they retain? Whom and what would they dump?

Things unfolded rapidly. Nelson's will appointed the heads of the universities of Kansas, Missouri and Oklahoma to handle the sale. They, in turn, named as trustees three Kansas Citians: developer J.C. Nichols, businessman and philanthropist William Volker and real estate man Herbert V. Jones. The trustees took bids, due in early July.

The bids came from New York newspaperman Frank Gannett; from the owner of *The Nashville Tennessean*, Luke Lea; from *The Star*'s old foe, Frederick Bonfils of *The Denver Post*; from Clyde Reed, publisher of *The Parsons Sun* in southeast Kansas; from H.V. Jones, owner of *The Minneapolis Journal*; from a Michigan newspaper group, and from Kansas Citian Walter Dickey, who detested *The Star*. There was one more bidder — a group of more than 80 *Star* employees led and largely staked by Irwin Kirkwood.

The bids were taken and bidders interviewed by the trustees on July 9, 1926, a Friday. All weekend the trustees debated. Staff members of *The Star* worried. At least two of the bidders openly despised *The Star*. Most of the other bidders were from another city. Hope lay with the Kirkwood group, yet in the beginning their effort looked like a long shot. Odds had improved, but would they be enough? Were they going to be sold to a sworn enemy? To a boss headquartered hundreds of miles away?

The scene at 18th and Grand on Monday afternoon, July 12, was recalled by longtime theater critic and Sunday editor E. B. Garnett:

"We at the office waited anxiously for Mr. Kirkwood and Mr. Seested to return from some listening post they had set up in the Kansas City Club. The big oak door of the city room swung open. A large man wearing an immaculate tan silk suit and broad-brimmed Panama hat entered.

"It was Irwin Kirkwood, all smiles. We rushed forward as he went to his desk. He greeted us before he had time to sit down.

" 'It's all right boys. We have bought *The Star*.' "

Applause came from every corner of the newsroom, Garnett recalled, from copy editors and department editors, reporters and clerks. All rushed forward and most simply said, "Congratulations."

The Star, for which Kirkwood and associates had offered $11 million — second highest on record for an American newspaper at the time— would be owned by its employees, or at least some of them, for the next half-century. Kirkwood, in fact, held the majority of the stock — one share more than half. The paper happily published letters and telegrams from Kansas Citians and other pleased that the newspaper would continue to be locally owned.

Kirkwood's role was enormous. Two and one-half million dollars in cash was raised in the effort, and $8.5 million borrowed from the New England National Bank. Given that Kirkwood had more than 50 percent of the shares, it can be assumed he tossed in at least $1.25 million, which would have been possible for a man who had $2 million of his own and was receiving $2 million from Laura Nelson Kirkwood's estate. Most of the shares were distributed by the thousands among Kirkwood and the board members. Rank-and-file employees often received shares numbering only in the single digits.

In years to come, for each major stockholder a life insurance policy was taken out so the stock could be bought back when he or she died. For every stockholder, use of the stock as collateral for a loan was banned; the paper didn't want a foreclosing bank to own a piece of *The Star*. The idea was to keep *The Star* in the family. It worked for half a century.

The newspaper was officially transferred to the Irwin S. Kirkwood Employee Trust. Before July ended, however, Walter S. Dickey sued to overturn the sale, claiming he and other outside bidders failed to receive necessary information about *The Star* properties, and that Kirkwood and other *Star* managers had engineered the process for their benefit.

Dickey was in high dudgeon. Earlier that month, as the bids were coming due, Dickey had sued *The Star* for libel for quoting a former Missouri governor as calling Dickey a political fraud. That suit went nowhere. In 1928, Dickey's separate action to overturn the sale finally was dismissed by the Missouri Supreme Court and in February 1929 the United States Supreme Court refused to review it. Any doubt about ownership of the newspaper was swept away, and the proceeds of the sale were free to be used for stocking a new museum of art.

Kirkwood exercised a genial oversight. He acted, according to George Longan, as "a great harmonizer." Longan recalled how the top officers gathered at *The Star* on Saturday evenings while the Sunday paper was produced and "after the work was well in hand, he would say, 'Well, let's go out to the house.' "

There, at Oak Hall, the men would discuss problems and argue over differences, eventually settling them.

Yet a new shock awaited. Barely a year after leading the purchase, on Aug 29, 1927, Irwin Kirkwood died of a heart attack in Saratoga Springs, N.Y., where he had gone to sell some of his thoroughbred horses. His death stunned *The Star* and the friends who were with him Saratoga Springs.

The editors and managers who had run *The Star* in Nelson's last years and

"Family" matters

Employee ownership endured half a century, and *The Star* stayed so much "in the family" that outsiders were almost never hired for management or other senior jobs.

Instead, *Star* reporters and editors worked their way up, making their way by their skills, longevity or both. The company was run by a board of directors; combined, its members owned most of the stock. The board decided when and to which employee stock would be offered.

In keeping with Nelson's design when the building at 18th and Grand was constructed, no company officer had a private office. The president's desk was in the newsroom. The institution was run by conference among directors, instead of by mandate from the chief.

The plan succeeded admirably in the first decades. Luckily for the new owners, profits in the first five years, from 1926 to 1931, were handsome. As a result, they were used to pay off the mortgage early. The debt to the trustees was eliminated in 1939, four years before the original date.

Heavy rolls of paper moved on a miniature rail system.

Bigger paper, bigger plant

"For once and for all time, The Star *is determined to have room and light and air and safety. It has been crowding itself out of house and home continuously for 30 years."*

— "About the *Kansas City Star* Office," booklet published in 1911 by *The Star*

The newspaper's home at 18th Street and Grand Avenue was designed with expansion in mind. It could accept twice the press capacity with which it began and double the staff in the newsroom. Eleven thousand square feet in the basement and about 8,000 square feet more on the top floor were reserved for future needs. Six hundred fifty employees worked there the building's first year.

It did not take long for everything to fill up. By 1923, all three floors of the brick-faced Italian Renaissance-style building were expanded to the north.

By 1915 average circulation was nudging 200,000 and the next year press capacity was increased again. At the same time, 21 new linotype machines were ordered.

In 1926, circulation reached 240,000. That same year, all new presses were ordered. They were fed from reels in a sub-basement, for which *The Star* built its own tiny rail network with carts to move rolls of newsprint into position.

New presses, ordered by the new employee owners, were installed in the late 1920s.

through the family succession now were fully in charge. Company stock was made available to more employees, and dividends were increased to help them pay for their shares.

Vowing to keep doing what it had been doing, *The Star* noted: "This newspaper is in a peculiar relationship to Kansas City. In an unusual way, it has come to be a part of the family life as well as of the community life of its readers.

"Nearly half its income goes to the city for the furtherance of art," the editorial continued. "The community has a unique concern in its future."

Replacing Kirkwood at the top of the year-old employee ownership was August F. Seested, 63, the immigrant from Prussia who had started at *The Star* in 1881, the second year of its existence. He was 17 years old when Nelson hired him, and his first job was to collect overdue bills from subscribers. Seested rose to become Nelson's right-hand man, in charge of making sure *The Star* made money.

"Gus," Nelson was supposed to have said to him one day, "when I become president, you'll be secretary of the treasury."

Laura Nelson Kirkwood once told a reporter that her father had not been "a great business man."

"He had no talent for business details," she said. "Mr. Seested relieved him of those."

Seested played a huge role in the newspaper's growth and success. Yet the

Seested era, like Kirkwood's, was over quickly. He died in October 1928 and once more the employee ownership had to appoint a new head man. This time, it chose George Longan, the first of several longtime newsroom hands to lead the company. Longan had joined *The Star* in the early 1900s and served as city editor, assistant managing editor and managing editor. He would remain at the helm until World War II.

Not long after the new Kansas City Star Co. was organized and its board found its feet, the decision came to save money by folding Laura Kirkwood's pet project, the Sunday magazine. It was replaced by a Sunday section featuring well-reproduced photographs from around the city and the world using the gravure printing process. In 1926, the newspaper ordered new, faster presses from Goss, the company's largest order to that date. In the order was a press capable of printing the Sunday color comics. By 1928 the presses were installed and proudly announced in the pages of the paper.

Breaking with past practice, *The Star* conspicuously began printing news from the other side in certain questions, usually political campaigns. By the middle 20th century that had become standard procedure for most mainstream newspapers, but the practice marked a clean break from the Daily W.R. Nelson. Often, the colonel refused to treat equally any position to which he was opposed, saying, "If people don't like my paper they can buy another."

Nelson's successors in the employee ownership disagreed. In the city elections of 1924, both sides got space for their views. In the 1928 presidential campaign *The Star* made a point of giving plenty of space and fair coverage to the campaign of Al Smith, the Democrat whom *The Star* opposed. In 1930, it even made a courtesy bow to the work of H.F. McElroy, Thomas Pendergast's handpicked city manager — before lambasting him for allowing Pendergast's concrete company so much of the work on new civic structures.

University of Missouri President Walter Williams, in an article for the paper's 50th anniversary in 1930, wrote: "It has mellowed somewhat and humanized since the men who make *The Star* own *The Star*.... The glow of *The Star* is gentler, but it is none the less vivid and provocative." Editor Henry J. Haskell, leader of the editorial page who was present long before and long after Nelson's death, acknowledged the calmer aspect in an interview with a scholar in the late 1940s.

In most respects, however, *The Star* continued as it had under Nelson — riding 35 years of momentum.

Continuing in the footsteps of Nelson — who in the 1890s commissioned William Allen White to study gas rates and write articles condemning the high cost of gas paid by Kansas Citians — *The Star* went after the Cities Service gas company. The first in a series of articles was published Sept. 18, 1930, the newspaper's 50th anniversary. What better way to celebrate a birthday than to fire up another crusade?

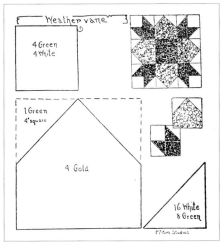

Printed Jan. 5, 1929

An inspiration for quilters

In 1928, *The Star* began printing quilt patterns submitted by readers and redrawn by staff artists. They were a standing feature in the newspaper's weekly publication, *The Weekly Kansas City Star* — later named *The Kansas City Star Farmer* — until that publication was ended in 1961. The weekly paper had subscribers not only throughout Missouri and Kansas but also Arkansas and Oklahoma. Of the 410 farms in Wallace County in far western Kansas, for example, 346 subscribed to the *Weekly Star* in 1938. For quilters in rural areas, *The Star*'s patterns were a continuing inspiration. Today, quilters worldwide consider The Kansas City Stars premium patterns to collect. When they were first published the patterns often reflected the tenor of their times. In the barnstorming days of the late 1920s and 1930s, aviation designs were popular. World War II brought patriotic patterns named The Army Star and Roads to Berlin. In 1999 the newspaper began collecting the patterns in a series of books.

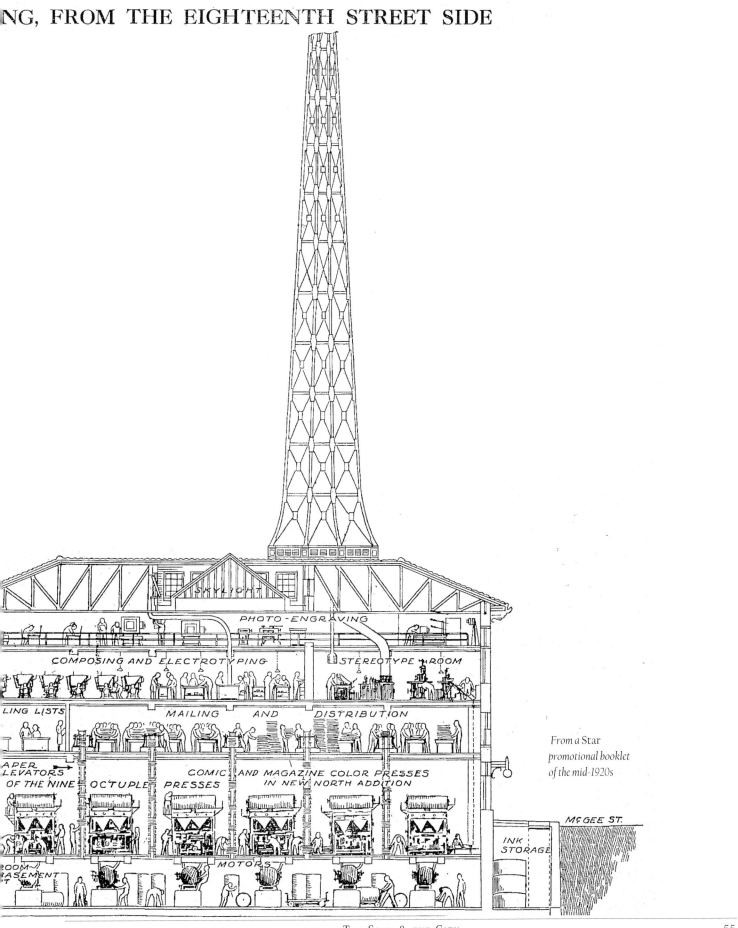

*From a Star
promotional booklet
of the mid-1920s*

"Gas Hold on City: The Users Pay While the Doherty Interests Adjust and Build Up Their Business," the front-page headline said that day. "Profit All Down the Line."

All this *The Star* laid at the feet of Henry L. Doherty, a New York-based petroleum tycoon and ruthless competitor who amassed a personal fortune partly through his genius in devising rates and in promotion. Doherty's Cities Service Co. controlled Kansas City Gas along with electrical utilities, gas companies and oil properties in more than a score of states and several foreign countries. Cities Service also sold gas appliances to promote use of its product.

Through spring 1930, *The Star* subjected Doherty to withering fire for charging Kansas Citians rates for natural gas that the newspaper deemed exorbitant. One Doherty company sold gas to another, the paper charged and multiplied the eventual cost to Kansas City customers.

"A 95-Cent Penalty," *The Star* headlined Sept. 21, 1930. "Typical Gas User Here Pays Much Above the Average Rate of Eleven Cities: The Doherty Gouge of its Consumers Here Shown Clearly...."

One of the counts in Henry Doherty's libel suits against The Star *cited this cartoon by S. J. Ray, published July 6, 1931.*

It was a full-fledged crusade that would have pleased Nelson. *The Star* employed almost daily news articles, editorials, cartoons and photos to push for lower gas rates. Doherty himself was made the centerpiece of the attacks. One editorial compared him by inference with Captain Kidd.

Meanwhile, Kansas banned the sale of some Cities Service securities.

Doherty had amassed his empire through hard work and disgust with obstacles. With its articles, *The Star* was erecting a bothersome obstacle.

Infuriated, the tycoon fired back. In mid-1931 he filed three libel suits asking damages of $54 million — at the time the largest libel action filed against any U.S. newspaper. Trying to use every angle, Doherty beseeched the postmaster general to bar *The Star* from the mail, and told the U.S. Commerce Department that the governor of Kansas had threatened to place some Cities Service subsidiaries into receivership. Doherty believed the state actions were a result of *The Star*'s prodding.

"I hope to be able to help free the people and the business interests of the Middle West from the buccaneering and terroristic tactics of *The Kansas City Star*," he wrote.

Close on the heels of the suit, Doherty bought a half-interest in *The Kansas City Journal-Post* from Walter Dickey, the onetime multimillionaire whose fortune was depleted by his spending on the newspaper. *The Journal* and *Post* bled money. Dickey's own resources had their limits. In 1928, he restricted publication to one edition a day, calling his remaining afternoon paper *The Journal-Post*. By 1931 Dickey had lost what some estimated as $15 million in the effort to beat *The Star*. He died within the year.

In Doherty, *The Journal* had a half-owner who detested *The Star* as much as Dickey had. Leaving the newspaper at least nominally in control of Dickey's son and son-in-law, Doherty styled himself a contributing editor with the right to publish anything he desired. Thus, Doherty kept up the drumbeat, trying to drive *The Star* out of business. Before long, Doherty bought out Dickey's heirs. *The Journal* continued to lower advertising rates to try to draw merchants into his paper and out of *The Star*. All his efforts failed, and he backed out of active involvement in 1938, dying at the end of 1939. At the time, Doherty reportedly controlled more than $1 billion in assets.

The last of his lawsuits was dismissed in 1939 and his estate sold *The Journal* in 1941. It would close the next year.

Against the machine

Meanwhile, Kansas City was deep into its most fabled and notorious era. If the Depression was hurting everyday business, the underground was flourishing. On the southeast edge of downtown, nightclubs and houses of prostitution flourished with the entertainment provided by hot jazz bands. Police looked the other way as organized crime raked in profits. A series of kidnapings of prominent people and the attendant publicity, along with a deadly shootout between law enforcement officials and gunmen at Union Station, put Kansas City on the country's crime map. In March 1934, hoodlums shoot four persons to death near the polls on election day.

The name that characterized this wide-open era for crime and corruption was that of the onetime Democratic factional leader who now ruled much of the city — Thomas J. Pendergast. He gained that power partly because of the work of reformers backed by *The Star*, efforts that quite clearly backfired.

Since the 1910s civic reformers and *The Star* had argued that Kansas City could be run better, cleaner and more efficiently if its governing structure were altered. Since the 19th century, Kansas City had been run by a mayor and 32-member board of aldermen, divided into two houses. *The Star*'s Nelson and others pushed to change that to a commission form, a nonpartisan one with council members elected at large. The aim was to eliminate both territorial and partisan disputes.

In the early 1920s that movement transformed itself as academics and progressives promoted a city manager form of government. Day-to-day administration of the city would be handled by a professional city manager, free of political taint and hired by a council chosen in a nonpartisan election. The mayor's powers would be reduced to those of any other council member. William Volker and other reformers — among them the leadership of The Star — believed this would bring a new era of professionalism to government, diminish patronage and

Henry J. Haskell, one of William Rockhill Nelson's favorites, was an erudite writer who won two Pulitzer Prizes — one in 1933 for commentary on national affairs, one in 1944 for thoughtful essays on national and international conditions. As editor for much of the first half of the century, he oversaw The Star's editorial page.

In 1931, A.B. Macdonald won the Pulitzer Prize for solving a murder case in the Texas panhandle. A reporter in Kansas City since 1892, Macdonald's forte was investigations. He helped expose the quackery of J.R. Brinkley, the "goat gland doctor" of Milford, Kan.

The dream realized

A decade and a half after the death of William Rockhill Nelson, his dream of a public art display finally took shape in the early 1930s. Nelson's will had called for proceeds from sale of *The Star*, which fetched $11 million in 1926, to create the William Rockhill Nelson Trust. Income from it was to be used to buy painting, sculptures, tapestries and rare books — art for Kansas City. According to his will, the presidents of the universities of Kansas, Missouri and Oklahoma were to name three trustees to oversee the collection.

The building to house this art was built by gifts from the estates of Nelson's wife, Ida Nelson; his daughter, Laura Nelson Kirkwood and her husband, Irwin Kirkwood; from his family lawyer, Frank Rozelle; and from a Kansas Citian who died in 1911, Mary McAfee Atkins. She was unrelated to the Nelson family.

The Nelson Gallery of Art — today's Nelson-Atkins Museum — arose on Nelson's Oak Hall property after his sprawling limestone mansion was razed.

Ground was broken for the gallery's east wing, named for Mary Atkins, in April 1931. Despite its name, it was connected to and undistinguishable from the rest of the gallery. In it were placed the 33 galleries and period rooms that greeted visitors at the public opening in December 1933. Six more galleries opened in the west wing in 1941 and the first floor was fully occupied by 1949.

The gallery realized Nelson's long quest to improve his surroundings — namely the city he called home. On an extended visit to Europe in the middle 1890s, he was taken by the art of the old masters. He bought copies of famous paintings turned out by a studio in Florence, had them shipped them to Kansas City and donated them to the school district, which put them on view at the public library. That collection was called the Western Gallery of Art.

For the new art gallery, collecting began in 1930, and by the

The art gallery under construction in 1932.

opening more than $4 million had been spent on more than 4,000 works of art.

The trustees appointed under Nelson's will chose experts to make the selections. They were barred, however, from acquiring works by artists dead less than 30 years. To add works from the 20th century, the gallery formed the Friends of Art to amass a second fund that got around Nelson's restriction.

Rozelle court, named for Nelson's lawyer, who left money for the gallery. Originally open, it has since been enclosed.

party influence, and thus reduce the influence of machine politicians.

In 1924 the idea was adopted by Kansas City voters. Surprisingly, the Pendergast organization supported the idea. The boss knew that if he controlled a majority of the council he could name the city manager. Besides, a smaller council meant fewer officeholders to manipulate. Like the reformers, Pendergast got his wish. Pendergast's candidates dominated the council and they hired the boss's own man, Henry F. McElroy, who settled in at the city manager's desk. With general direction from 1908 Main Street, Pendergast's nondescript headquarters, McElroy proceeded to execute the wishes of the machine.

McElroy

The reform made it possible for a single faction to dominate everything and dominate it did. Organization favorites got jobs made possible by a bond issue that launched a vast public building program. It spurred construction of a new city hall and courthouse, Municipal Auditorium, the paving of Brush Creek, and street and park projects throughout the area.

The Police Department came under control of the city administration for the first time in decades; the courts threw out a law that had kept it under state control to insulate it from local pressure. As police looked the other way, gambling and rackets thrived. At election time, the Pendergast machine used roughhouse tactics to get its way, much as it had in the 1910s .

Reform forces stewed for years until one spring afternoon in 1932, when the women of the Government Study Club luncheon attendees heard this from the rabbi of Temple B'Nai Jehudah:

"You've turned your city over to a gang and given it into the hands of crooks and racketeers because you've been asleep."

Rabbi Samuel S. Mayerberg was firing the first public shot of the incipient anti-machine campaign.

Mayerberg

"Kansas City has the finest city charter in the United States," Mayerberg said. "If it were administered as it was intended, we would have an ideal city government."

Not only were city workers solicited for campaign contributions and some fired because they were not of the right party or faction, Mayerberg said, elections themselves were being stolen. He derided "the kidnapers of election officials and the stuffers of the ballot boxes."

City Manager McElroy, he contended, "is guilty of violation of the law, and if we had a country prosecutor who was not part of the political machine, he himself would bring the charge against this man!"

Star reporter Alvin S. McCoy, who would one day win a Pulitzer prize for his reporting about a scandal in Kansas state government, was new to the staff that year. According to ex-*Star* reporter William M. Reddig in his book, *Tom's Town*, that meeting of the Government Study Club ordinarily might have been ignored by the paper. Its members, however, were the wives of prominent Kansas Citians. McCoy

Landon's their man

By the 1930s, William Rockhill Nelson's long-ago pledge that *The Star* would remain independent but never neutral lay in tatters. Nelson himself helped the process along with his devotion to Theodore Roosevelt and the Progressive Party. In local elections, *The Star* tended to favor Republican candidates if for no other reason than they stood in opposition to the dominant political machines, which were Democratic.

In 1936, the leaders of *The Star* played an active and central role in the nomination of a Republican candidate for president, Kansas' own Gov. Alfred M. Landon.

Landon had cut his political teeth in the Theodore Roosevelt and Progressive Party campaign of 1912, made his own fortune in oil and gas in the 1920s and won allies throughout Kansas as campaign manager for another Republican in 1928. In 1932, he was elected governor and re-elected in 1934, running a mildly progressive administration that saw state spending per capita drop. Amid the wave of President Franklin Roosevelt's New Deal, Landon was one of only a few Republican governors in office. His administration's success in controlling expenses, his re-election in the midst of the Depression and his middle-American manner gained him notice as a possible GOP contender against Roosevelt.

What propelled him to the nomination, however, was a whirlwind publicity campaign in newspapers and magazines, a substantial part of it orchestrated by *The Star*'s managing editor, Roy Roberts, and its Kansas bureau manager, Lacy Haynes. From

Gov. Alf Landon of Kansas, right, talked politics with a rumpled Roy Roberts, then managing editor of The Star *and adviser to the GOP presidential candidate. This meeting was at Union Station in September 1936, during the campaign.*

his days as *The Star*'s Washington correspondent, Roberts had gained a good working knowledge of national politics. Haynes, because he represented the newspaper with the biggest circulation in Kansas, had wielded clout in Topeka for years. Both clearly understood newspapers. By pointing out to the nation that Kansas had balanced its budget and cut spending while New Deal programs did the opposite, they fixed Republicans' attention on Landon as "The Great Economizer" and "The Kansas Coolidge."

Soon, publisher William Randolph Hearst had reporters for his nationwide newspaper chain examining and then writing glowing accounts about Landon. With the boom under way, Haynes, Roberts and Henry J. Haskell were often at his side, advising and helping craft speeches. Landon won the GOP nomination, having come to the national stage within a matter of months.

That November, Roosevelt and the New Deal overwhelmed not only Landon but also many sitting Republican members of Congress. Kansans even chose a Democrat for governor. If there had been any doubt about *The Star*'s stand on national politics, it was now erased. Roberts — who would be managing editor another decade and president of the Kansas City Star Co. after that — remained a power in the Republican Party. In the minds of many of its readers, the paper would be identified with the GOP for decades to come.

knew that, and also had been impressed by Mayerberg. So he sat through his talk and turned in his story.

McCoy's account appeared on the front page that afternoon, along with an item about the rabbi's visit with the Ministerial Alliance. Urging them to take leadership of an anti-machine movement, Mayerberg said:

"I know of 35 speakeasies operating in this city. I know of 50 places where tickets on horse races are sold. It is a hidden evil, well fortified and protected. It strikes at the decency of Kansas City."

If you wanted it, Kansas City had it

As the railroad and population center of nearly everything between Chicago and the Rockies, Kansas City saw a considerable body of travelers and visitors in the 1920s and 1930s. One of the biggest tourist attractions — and of no small interest to many residents — was the city's thriving vice. Speakeasies prospered throughout Prohibition and alcohol flowed 24 hours a day during and after the ban. Prostitution was open, gambling prevalent and drug trafficking considerable. Much of the vice was directly or tacitly supported by the political machine of Thomas J. Pendergast.

As Lawrence J. Larsen and Nancy J. Huston found in their book *Pendergast!* the boss did more than look the other way. He actively promoted the gambling as an economic boon for the city.

Although it was illegal in most of the country, gambling of all kinds was available: Dice, cards and crap games, sports betting, slot machines and bingo. Betting on the horses was popular, too, and Pendergast participated avidly. Nightclubs offered booze and women, and some of the waitresses wore little or no clothing. Prostitutes were easily available.

Most of the city's neighborhoods remained respectable and quiet; even at the height of the wide-open era in the 1930s, the bulk of vices were found Downtown or nearby.

Where it occurred, vice was obvious. The infamous Chesterfield Club with its unclothed waitresses recruited from houses of prostitution was one block from the federal courthouse. The houses themselves lined 14th Street. Often, there was a distinctive music — bands of white musicians and black, playing a bouncy kind of jazz.

Several of the black performers would become internationally famous. William — later Count — Basie and a young Charlie

In 1939, Kansas City Journal *photographer Jack Wally, with the aid of fellow newsman John Cameron Swayze, sneaked a tiny camera into the Baltimore Recreation gambling hall and covertly snapped away at horsetrack bettors, card players and others. The photographs were published in* Life *magazine.*

Parker, both graduates of Kansas City groups, have long symbolized the quality of music called Kansas City jazz.

Benny Moten's band on the Fairyland Park stage in 1931. William — later Count — Basie stood in the front row, second from left.

In an atmosphere of municipal abandon, jazz groups played at clubs like the Spinning Wheel at 12th Street at Troost Avenue, above, the Reno Club, below left, and the Harlem Nite Club, below right.

The question of Kansas City's decency had, indeed, been raised across the country. Events painted an ugly picture in the national consciousness of the 1930s. Gambling flourished, as did prostitution.

Then there was the violent crime. Kansas City's was striking, even in an era marked by highly publicized mobsters and other hoodlums.

High-profile kidnappings abounded. In 1930, Katz Drug co-founder Michael Katz was driving on Ward Parkway when a car driven by two men forced his car to the curb. They covered Katz's head with a hood and demanded ransom. In 1931, dress manufacturer Nell Donnelly and her chauffeur were kidnapped at gunpoint from the driveway of her home on Oak Street. In 1933, City Manager McElroy's daughter, Mary, was taken from the family home and kept in a hideout near Shawnee. In the cases of Katz and McElroy, thousands of dollars in ransom were paid. Donnelly and chauffeur were freed before money changed hands. All victims survived.

In June 1933, as law enforcement officers were returning escaped convict Frank Nash to Leavenworth penitentiary, gunmen appeared near their car in the parking lot of Union Station. Shots were fired, Nash and four of the officers were killed, and the killers got away. The much-publicized case was used by J. Edgar Hoover to strengthen his fledgling Bureau of Investigation and make it the FBI.

As the 1934 city election neared, *The Star*, arm in arm with some young reformers, Republicans and anti-Pendergast Democrats, put up a ticket for mayor and council. Defeat was nearly certain for the reformers, but machine politicians made certain the vote was not close. Illegal registrants and voters added tens of thousands of votes to the machine totals.

Polling place intimidation surely added more. Some would-be voters were cursed by precinct workers and run off before they could cast ballots. Thugs roamed the streets, injuring dozens. At one precinct on East 24th Street, they barged in and killed a poll worker. At another on Swope Parkway three people were shot to death.

Star reporter Justin Bowersock saw the violence first-hand. Accompanied by two adherents of the reform ticket, Bowersock was driving his car as the three looked for repeat voters. At a polling place on East Eighth Street, they saw three cars loaded with men and women about to leave. Following those cars toward another polling place at Ninth Street and Troost Avenue, Bowersock's vehicle was blocked by three other automobiles. Their occupants approached, leveling firearms at Bowersock and his companions.

They grabbed the reporter by the necktie, pulled him from the car and struck him on the back of the head, once with the butt of a pistol and a second time with a fist. He was able to get away. Bowersock ran around a corner and entered another vehicle driven by reform sympathizers. The car raced away, followed by one of the attacker's cars. Bowersock and his rescuers arrived at the McGee Street entrance

of *The Star*. He was pursued to the door by one of his attackers, but made it safely inside.

In *Tom's Town*, Reddig described the scene in the newsroom as Bowersock — his face blanched, hair tousled and forehead bloodied — rushed in.

"They're after me," Bowersock shouted. "They're trying to kill me!"

Several reporters and editors ducked, then realized his assailants had not entered the building, much less the newsroom on the second floor.

His rescuer, meanwhile, drove to Union Station, and took a taxicab from there to reform ticket headquarters.

Bowersock's original companions were badly beaten after the reporter escaped. They were found inside Bowersock's bullet-riddled car, unable to move but alive.

Fulminating, someone cranked out an editorial for Page One of the next morning's *Times*, headlined "The Shame of It!"

"The gangsters ran wild because they knew the police would do nothing to stop them," the editorial said. "Cars without license numbers, loaded with armed men, roamed about the streets at will — and the police looked the other way."

The next issue of *The Star*, in another front-page editorial, lamented:

Aftermath of the Union Station massacre, June 17, 1933.

How votes were delivered

Two *Star* reporters investigating a 1936 election found instance after instance of questionable vote padding and of "ghost voters." Two voters' addresses would have been on the bank or in the middle of the Blue River, above right. Others were registered from an empty cafe, right. Ten voters were registered at a feed mill and grain elevator on Manchester Avenue.

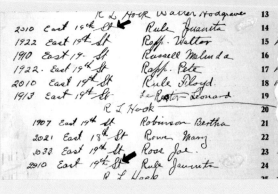

Left: Precinct judges wrote voters' names in the left column at registration time, last name first. Juanita Rule's appears twice. The right column contained the voter's signature. Rule's is signed twice, the second time, oddly, with her last name first.

"All over the United States today, where the news is carried by the Associated Press, people will be asking, 'What sort of city is Kansas City?'

"We talk about advertising Kansas City to the country. Then the constituted authorities, the police department, allow gangsters to run wild.

"These bloody facts go out as an invitation to people to come here to live and do business! This sort of thing cannot go on."

Yet go on it did. In July, the boss of Kansas City's underworld, Johnny Lazia, was gunned down as he stepped from his chauffeured car outside his midtown apartment. Who killed him has never been determined.

Pendergast's wide-open town was becoming a long-term embarrassment, if not a clear and present danger, to more and more Kansas Citians. *The Star* doubled its efforts.

Expecting the same voting illegalities in the 1936 election, the newspaper assigned two reporters to scrutinize the rolls. They found 270,000 registered voters, about half again as many as would be typical in a city of 400,000.

Twenty-eight names were registered at 1305 Grand Ave., a two-story building housing a paint and glass company on the first floor. There the reporters found no residents, and nothing on the second floor. At a funeral parlor, they found one occupant where 17 voters were registered. Two voters gave an address that would have been on the banks of the Blue River or in its current, next to the Manchester Avenue bridge. On East Ninth Street, an address marking only a dusty, empty storeroom claimed four registrants.

On voting rolls, they found the same name at different addresses, and sometimes the same name at the same address listed twice. At one polling place, a Juanita Rule was registered twice, last name first. On the voter signature lines, one was signed "Juanita Rule," the second "Rule, Juanita," just the way it had been entered by precinct election judges at registration time. The examples went on, photographed and published in shocking sameness in *The Star*. The evidence was graphic and clear: Kansas City's rolls were extensively padded.

On his way out, Pendergast waited to be driven away from his trial in 1939.

In 1939, Pendergast and his machine began to crumble. Public indignation, helped along by *The Star*'s revelations, was one reason, but only one of many. The immediate cause of Pendergast's fall was the boss himself.

Addicted to betting on horses but not very good at it, Pendergast had poured hundreds of thousands of dollars into losing wagers. When his funds ran low, he offered to influence an insurance settlement with the state of Missouri in the insurance company's favor. In return, the company handed Pendergast $440,000, of which he kept $315,000. In 1936, agents of the U.S. Treasury Department began sniffing around the edges of the matter. Later, the governor of Missouri heard about it and called for a federal probe. Federal prosecutors zeroed in and a grand jury indicted Pendergast for failing to pay income taxes on the bribe. In May 1939, he pleaded guilty and was sent to federal prison in Leavenworth.

In articles, editorials and cartoons, *The Star* boosted a "clean sweep" campaign in 1940 — in which the symbol was broom that would clean out City Hall. A reform ticket was elected. The wide-open town began to close some of its doors.

War, strike and a big man ascends

As in the rest of America, World War II was a watershed for Kansas City. For the first time in Kansas City history, heavy industry opened its doors to make planes, engines and armaments for the war effort. More than 40,000 workers

In an S. J. Ray cartoon, reform workers with their symbolic clean-sweep brooms surrounded an outmanned machine politician at City Hall.

moved to the area to take all the new jobs at Pratt & Whitney and at North American Aviation and at ordnance plants. Aviation and electronics schools kept the city hopping with servicemen and Union Station handled more trains than ever before. At *The Star*, the needs of the armed services removed young men from the ranks; a bronze service roll lists more than 250 names from editorial, business and mechanical departments. For the first time in *Star* history, women entered the newsroom to cover regular news beats.

With all the war news to report, *The Star* faced the unhappy circumstance of a sharply restricted supply of newsprint. Among other things, paper mills converted to production of war-related items. One of the key ingredients in transforming wood pulp into paper also was a key ingredient in explosives.

Not only did *The Star* trim the number of news columns, but also it had to reduce or reject advertising, costing it untold amounts of revenue. In 1942, it dropped the Sunday rotogravure section begun 16 years earlier. By war's end, the paper shortage was forcing the paper to turn down new subscribers.

When peace arrived in 1945, *The Star*'s hometown literally leaped out of its restraints. Fueled by the GI bill, returning members of the services went back to college, started families and bought homes in new suburbs such as Prairie Village and Leawood. In postwar Kansas City newspaper delivery routes sprawled ever farther from *The Star*'s plant, complicating delivery of two newspapers a day. New weekly newspapers sprang up in the suburbs, aiming to nibble away at *The Star*'s dominance of the Kansas City readership, which had become complete when its last competitor, the nearly century-old *Kansas City Journal*, folded on March 31, 1942.

The great postwar economic recovery opened an era when *The Star* made huge profits and achieved record average circulation, well over 300,000. Nevertheless, paper shortages persisted. Wanting to guarantee a reliable stream of paper, *The Star*'s board of directors bought a paper mill in Wisconsin, one of several acquisitions by the company that seemed wise at the time.

Amid the postwar excitement, labor unions felt emboldened, too. In January 1947, *The Star*'s pressmen went on strike in sympathy with delivery agents. For the first time in its history, *The Star* was unable to publish. The strike lasted two weeks and in the end the union won a pay raise and a guarantee of no reprisals from the company. Publication resumed in early February.

Meanwhile, perhaps from the stress of the strike, *The Star*'s president, Earl McCollum, suffered a heart attack and died. Quickly, the board of directors chose his replacement, as always from the current leadership.

The new president had appeared in that brief talking movie, the one produced in the newsroom in 1929. Then the newly annointed managing editor, a bit portly, he popped in and out of scenes. He barked an order here — "We've got to make over the front page!" "That's a hell of a story!" — and consulted with the top brass

Longan

George Longan, who served capably as president of The Star *for 14 years, had one exceedingly memorable peccadillo: an aversion to the paper's using the word, "snake." He believed certain readers reacted badly to it. Reporters and editors remembered that and how they had to work hard sometimes to avoid using it.*

In October 1942, Longan suffered a heart attack as he drove into his driveway on Ward Parkway and died. He was replaced by Earl McCollum, the paper's business manager, who guided the paper through newsprint shortages and other economic constrictions of World War II. In 1947, McCollum faced a pressmen's and printers' walkout, worked through the first week of the strike and then became too ill to continue. He died a week later.

McCollum

there. In the final scene, he was directing a staff artist to create a photo spread. Just back from a long stint as Washington correspondent, he enjoyed the rough and tumble of politics. Observant newsman though he was, he loved being a mover and shaker in politics.

Eighteen years as managing editor had only heightened his confidence. Now, in early 1947, a big and energetic man certain of his place in Kansas City and the nation, Roy Allison Roberts was chosen president of *The Kansas City Star*.

Signs of the times

Left: Booming ownership of automobiles produced a healthy market for parts, like these tire chains advertised in 1929. Above: Jazz-era entertainment advertised in The Star, *December 1934.*

THE KA
LARGES
ORGAN

Under employee ownership, the newspaper's operations were extensively photographed. From the delivery of newsprint rolls to sidewalk elevators on Grand Avenue, above left, to selling advertisements on the first floor, above, Star operations were documented.
Left: Making plates for rotary presses required lots of heat to melt lead. Some of the heat was vented out by long tubes.

Top: Billed as the "largest individual newspaper organization in the world," The Star's carriers lined up with their vehicles for a photograph in 1932.

Left: In the packaging and distribution area, commonly called the "mailroom," papers were stacked by hand. On big days, when more than one press run was necessary, large crews labored to combine sections by hand.

Above: The newsroom had its own skylight.

1947 ~ 1976

GOOD TIMES, HARD TIMES

For much of spring 1951, torrents of rain fell across the central plains. Creeks overflowed and rivers crested above their banks through thousands of square miles in central and eastern Kansas. All that water took its natural course, moving downstream on the Kansas River toward its confluence with the Missouri. There sat the two Kansas Citys, protected by floodwalls and levees.

They weren't enough.

In the predawn hours of Friday, July 13, the Kansas River, commonly known as the Kaw, began pouring into the Argentine section of Kansas City, Kansas. By dawn, the Armourdale district was filling, the flood moving up Kansas Avenue. Residents, most of them working class, fled as the water advanced. Later that morning water crested the floodwall guarding the West Bottoms.

Packing plants, stockyards, warehouses and factories shut down, their workers getting out just in time, some through elevated cattle chutes. Before long, the lower stories of all those buildings were inundated. The upper stories poked up through what had become a great inland sea. The great flood of 1951 lapped at the bluffs of the two cities.

The Star set to work — every reporter, photographer and editor who could be mustered into service. Day after day, page after page and column after column in the morning *Times* and the afternoon *Star*, the newspaper covered the deluge.

For its extensive coverage, the newspaper won a special citation from the Pulitzer Prize committee. It was *The Star*'s first Pulitzer since 1944, and its first ever for news coverage of a local event. Its circulation past 300,000, the only metro daily left in Kansas City, owner of the city's only television station, and still proprietor of one of its largest radio stations, *The Star* sat atop Kansas City's media world.

And atop *The Star* sat Roy Allison Roberts, president and general manager, proud of his newspaper, his television and radio stations and equally proud of his

1947	
Population	
Kansas City, Mo.	440,000
Seven-county total	840,000
Average number of pages	52*
Average circulation	364,800
* Times and Star total	

Facing page: A Star *photographer captured the West Bottoms under water in July 1951.*

Roberts at the microphone of The Star's radio station in July 1950.

standing in the city and in the newspaper profession. He would be the only person from *The Star* named "Mr. Kansas City" by the Chamber of Commerce. He would be the only leader of *The Star* to be on the cover of *Time* magazine.

The day after the Kaw topped the floodwalls, civic leaders gathered at the Kansas City Club. They heard Corps of Engineers spokesmen call for rapid completion of the agency's dam-and-reservoir system to control flooding on the Kaw and its tributaries.

Among the speakers was Roy Roberts. "We ought to all go out of here with just one thought," he told the group. "Never again!" The next morning, those words topped a Page One editorial saying, "The time to rise and take action is now, today, this next week." A couple of weeks later, Roberts placed full-page ads in newspapers in New York City, Chicago, Washington and Detroit headlined, "You can't lick Kansas City!"

They bore Roberts' signature, just as the newspaper and the city bore his stamp.

"I'll have the biggest damn funeral Kansas City has ever seen," *Time* quoted him as saying. "They'll all come out to see their old master laid away."

'The man to see in Kansas City'

Roberts liked to do things big. He had all the swagger of William Rockhill Nelson, perhaps even more. Probably he exceeded Nelson in weight, nearing 300 pounds at one point in his career. In the newsroom, he loved to slap backs. Some of the men remembered he sometimes slapped too hard. Some of the women remembered that he popped their bra straps.

In the city and country he wanted to make kings. Politics was Roberts' chief joy, and *The Star* gave him lifelong entrée. Early in his career, as Jefferson City correspondent and then reporting from Washington, Roberts had shown an insider's savvy. Upon becoming managing editor of the paper in 1928 Roberts, with Lacy Haynes of *The Star's* Kansas bureau in Kansas City, Kan., influenced Kansas politics for years. He and Haynes were key members of group of Kansas publishers and politicians who beat the drums for Alf Landon and pushed him to the GOP presidential nomination in 1936, with its unhappy ending in the Roosevelt landslide. In 1952, Roberts pushed hard for the election of Dwight D. Eisenhower, who grew up in Kansas. That time the outcome for Roberts was happier.

Roberts joined the staff of *The Star* in 1909 as William Rockhill Nelson was reaching his partisan zenith. For Theodore Roosevelt and the Progressive cause, Nelson clearly cast aside his longstanding pledge of political independence. *The Star* dispatched reporters as political operatives far and wide through Missouri. Roberts was one of them, even bringing back news that Nelson did not want to hear: Woodrow Wilson was going to carry the state. Clearly, Roberts was captivated by the experience. He never lost his lust for politics. He was assigned

full time to the Washington bureau in 1915, and in 1928 was called back to Kansas City to become managing editor, top job in the news operation. In 1947, he was chosen president of the company.

A self-described "big, fat boy from Kansas," Roberts proved a loyal disciple of Nelson's way. Like Nelson, Roberts was a big, occasionally rumpled man. Like Nelson he was domineering in and out of the office — not to mention a believer in holding the line on salaries. And like Nelson, Roberts was robust, opinionated and quite willing to be one of the country's politically influential publishers and editors. In the postwar era no national magazine's article about Kansas City was complete without mention of Roberts and *The Star*.

In its cover article on Roberts in 1948, *Time* declared him "the man to see in Kansas City to get elected, to build a hospital, to get things into the paper and to

The television age

The biggest newspaper in town already owned one of the biggest radio stations, so with the advent of television, *The Star* wanted in. Roy Roberts took credit for pushing the idea through the newspaper's board of directors. In August 1949, WDAF-TV began broadcasting a test pattern and on Sept. 29 broke in with a live, remote broadcast of a banquet at Municipal Auditorium for President Harry S. Truman's new Democratic Party chairman, William Boyle.

Regular programming began Oct. 16, with a live broadcast from the American Royal. Shortly after *The Star* gained its broadcasting permit, the federal government halted issuance of any more until it could better control the process. That meant WDAF-TV was Kansas City's only station until 1953, when the moratorium was lifted. In that time, homes with televisions grew from an estimated 7,000 in 1949 to tens of thousands by 1950 to hundreds of thousands by 1953.

The immediacy of television was amply demonstrated to Kansas Citians in July 1951, when Kansas River floodwaters backed up along the old bed of Turkey Creek, covering Southwest Boulevard. There, floating debris struck a fuel tank, and the tank exploded. A hellish mix of flames and smoke rose from the mess.

For the first time, Kansas Citians did not have to wait for the next edition of *The Star* to see pictures of the event. If they had televisions, they could tune into WDAF and watch the fire live. The station's new headquarters, perched at 31st Street and Southwest Trafficway, gave its cameras a balcony seat and viewers an instant image of the blaze.

The new medium scooped print, an early hint of its potential to changed the landscape of how people saw their world. But on that day the prospect didn't worry the people who ran *The Star*. After all, they owned WDAF.

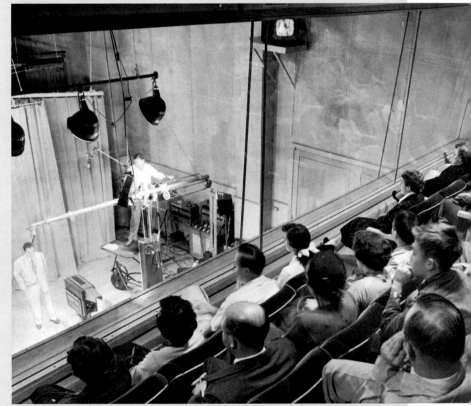

Top: WDAF's cameras at Municipal Auditorium for President Truman's banquet honoring William Boyle.
Above: From a studio balcony, spectators watched the magic of television as it was made.
Left: An early WDAF logo.

keep them out."

In 1949, only two years after his ascension to head the company, Roberts nudged the board of directors into the television age. An experimental shop was set up in a building nearby, and then a studio was constructed at 31ˢᵗ Street and Southwest Trafficway. Once the bugs were worked out, *The Star*'s WDAF-TV went on the air in late 1949.

Roberts fought and won battles with the government over taxes and labor relations, and oversaw an $8 million rebuilding of the production plant. Included were new presses capable of printing color in the daily paper.

The first time they did so was for the biggest paper *The Star* had ever printed, a 252-page Sunday edition June 4, 1950, commemorating the Centennial celebration that Kansas City staged that year. Besides four sections of regular news, sports, entertainment and features, the massive paper contained six sections exhaustively describing the history of the Kansas City area and the lives of Kansas Citians. Readers could peruse:

- "Debut of the Hannibal Bridge...How the Town Turned Out for This Occasion."
- "Along the Pioneer Cattle Trails...History of the Stock Yards Here."

The suburbs spring up: Prairie Village a-building in 1952, part of the phenomenal growth in northeast Johnson County in the 1940s and 1950s.

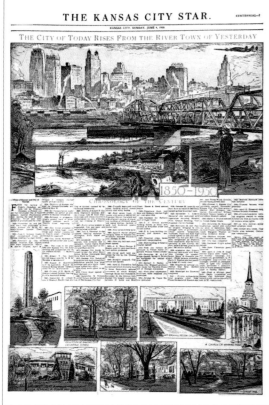

For The Star's special commemoration of Kansas City's Centennial celebration, sections printed in advance were stored in every nook and cranny.

Left: The first two full-color pages printed by the paper's regular presses.

- "Plane Travelers Meet at Municipal Air Terminal, Greatly Enlarged in Recent Improvement Program."
- "From Bustles to Bras…The Women's Page Editor Reviews Ten Decades of Fashions."

The first unit of the Goss Headliner press was moved into the Star *building in April 1949.*

Piled one on the other, it was calculated, the copies of that Sunday's paper would tower six miles high, "forty-six times the height of *The Star*'s television tower."

For all the paper's pride in its new presses and their color-printing capability, only two pages in the main newspaper that day contained color: The front page of the first Centennial section and an Emery Bird Thayer ad announcing a sale on blankets, sheets and pillowcases (As usual, the Sunday comics — printed on smaller pages on a separate press — and the ads within them were in color).

The big story was the city itself and its Centennial celebration.

One article detailed the "Thrills of a Century" pageant at brand-new Starlight theater in Swope Park, where actress Gloria Swanson presented a jeweled crown and scepter to the Centennial Queen. Another told of the industrial exposition at Municipal Auditorium, where "the industrial sinews of a mighty city were displayed in spectacular fashion."

The day's biggest headline told how the metropolitan area had reached 800,000 population, fueled by growth in the suburbs. The biggest leap since the 1940 census was in Mission Township — northeast Johnson County — which showed an astounding 250 percent growth.

The newspaper devoted a two-page advertising spread to itself, telling readers not only about its new presses and new television station, but also about its new paper-storage warehouse on the west side of Grand Avenue, its investment in an Alabama paper mill and the size and reach of its *Weekly Kansas City Star*.

Amid all this, the paper acknowledged, "*The Star* realizes the possibility of sounding boastful. Such is not its intention. Whatever pride *The Star* may feel is mingled with a sobering sense of responsibility and a spirit of gratitude that it has been privileged to witness, record and, in some measure, contribute to …the emergence of Kansas City."

Topping off the newspaper's effort for the Centennial was a 194-page book on the history of Kansas City written by two of *The Star*'s most thoughtful writers, Henry C. Haskell — son of Editor Henry J. Haskell — and Richard Fowler, an editorial writer. The volume was called *City of the Future*. Roy Roberts wrote the foreword, hailing the post-Pendergast reforms and clearly proud of the progress "of more than a decade as a city freed from political bondage."

Indeed, Kansas City was being run by officials backed by the Citizens Association, descendants of the 1930s reformers now entering their second decade of the Clean Sweep of machine politics. As city manager, they retained L.P. Cookingham, who supported the nonpartisan system of government, of parks and

The White House objects

Perhaps for the sheer joy of it, perhaps for the power he could wield, Roy Roberts loved the political life. He approached that life from a Republican point of view. One committed Democrat evidently felt strongly about Roberts and his newspaper. He was a longtime local politician who had risen to the ultimate office, the presidency. In 1950, Harry S. Truman was reading his copy of *The Star*'s Kansas City Centennial edition, and of the book *City of the Future*. As a product of the Pendergast organization, he had no love for the paper and its accusations of graft and vote-fraud.

He drafted several versions of a letter to Roberts containing his thoughts. They weren't happy ones.

"Dear Roy: — I have been going through your centennial editon. It is most interesting. I wish you'd had someone talk to me about some of the events mentioned and some of the pictures displayed.

"And now Roy, I'm going to tell you something that's good for

your soul. Your former boss Old Bill Nelson, in my book is lower than the belly of a snake!

"He left an Art Galery (sic) to make his peace with God Almighty...but I don't think he fooled Jehovah — and you can't either. The characters you've ruined and the people you've made unhappy have more chance of being right with God than have old Pigfaced Bill Nelson...."

"History will tell the tale," the president wrote, "and you and Big Pig Face Bill won't even be mentioned."

Truman signed, "President of the United States, in spite of you...."

The letter was never sent. A milder version, though still expressing annoyance, was mailed from Washington on June 17. It complained that *The Star*'s centennial history had treated H.F. McElroy "cruelly." He also had few good words to say about *City of the Future*.

Even toned down, the president made it obvious how he felt about Roberts and *The Star*.

of so much that *The Star* had fought for.

As the second half of the 20th century got under way, *The Star* and Roberts were at the top of their game.

In a matter of years, they would be shaken like never before.

The accusation: monopoly

In late June 1952, a subpoena arrived in the newspaper's headquarters at 18th and Grand. The United States Justice Department was seeking records — corporate records and advertising contracts of the newspaper and the television and radio stations — dating back to 1926, the first year of employee ownership. The antitrust division of the Justice Department wanted to take the evidence before a grand jury.

Management of *The Star* had some reason to worry, although it showed none of that in the newspaper. For three years, the Justice Department had been investigating newspapers around the country for antitrust violations in advertising. A Republican senator from Kansas, Frank Carlson, accused the Truman administration of a vendetta against the press for reporting various White

House scandals. In response to the subpoena, Roy Roberts said simply, "*The Star* has nothing to hide."

The bad news for the Star Co. arrived just after New Year's, in the waning days of the Truman Administration On Jan. 6, 1953, the grand jury indicted the company, Roberts, and advertising director Emil Sees for monopolizing advertising in the Kansas City area. An accompanying civil suit sought revocation of the Star Co.'s television and radio license.

"*The Star* will insist on an early trial," Roberts proclaimed, "confident that complete vindication will come from court and jury." He rejected any idea of a settlement, and participants recall Roberts' attacking the matter at every turn with bluster. Confidence turned to hubris.

As the trial unfolded, *The Star* printed voluminous accounts of testimony, favorable and unfavorable. Those thousands of printed words brought to the surface another dimension of *The Star*'s relationship with its city. No matter what it supported in its news and editorial columns and no matter how hard it fought corruption, the paper now was the only game in town.

Roberts hinted at an anti-*Star* prejudice by the Truman Administration. He pointed to what he called the Justice Department's zeal in prosecuting *The Star*, and compared it with a lack of interest by the same department in following up vote-fraud allegations made by the newspaper after local elections in 1946. In that campaign, Truman himself demanded defeat of the incumbent Democratic congressman from Kansas City, Roger Slaughter, who had battled with the Truman administration. Slaughter lost the August 1946 Democratic primary to a Truman-backed candidate. In some precincts the totals favoring Truman's candidate reeked of fraud like that unearthed in 1936. *The Star* mounted an investigation similar to its 1936 effort and found similar results — voters who reported addresses in burned-out buildings and corn patches, questionable counting procedures at the polls, election judges' filling out ballots for voters. The whole affair chilled relations between *The Star* and the then-new president. Was the antitrust action, announced only days before Truman was to leave office, a result?

"Despite this indictment," Roberts wrote, "there will be no relaxing in any degree of *The Star*'s efforts against ballot-box stuffing, ghost voting and all the other fraudulent devices to defeat the process of honest elections."

Before trial, the charges against Roberts were dropped, but the charges against his newspaper and its advertising director went forwad.

On NBC's "Meet the Press," the outgoing attorney general, James McGranery, denied politics played any part.

"We all claim politics of some sort when we get in trouble," he said, adding that complaints had come from "a number of advertisers in Kansas City — folks who were told they would have to advertise in a certain way or else."

The Justice Department action was encouraged by publishers of small

Organized labor and *The Star*

In the late 1940s organized labor felt *The Star* turning against it editorially. Things hadn't always been that way.

Nelson had gone both ways in labor matters, backing the strikers in the Homestead steel strike of 1892, yet backing the Santa Fe railroad against strikers the next year. Through the colonel's death, *The Star* had treated labor fairly even-handedly, but that began to change as the 20th Century wound on. After World War II, the newspaper supported the Taft-Hartley act, which crimped severely the power of unions.

In its own building, *The Star* tolerated unions, 14 of them by the late 1940s representing most operations except the news and business departments. Yet those relations became strained, too.

Clear evidence came in early 1947, when a strike by pressmen shut down the paper for 17 days. The walkout began the morning of January 17, when some of the paper's carriers picketed the building, seeking recognition of their union. *The Star*'s printers and pressmen refused to cross — even after the printers' union ordered its members back to work and even after slightly more than half the carriers won a court order ending the picketing. The strike ended February 3 after Roberts and the pressmen's union leader negotiated a settlement that gave the pressmen a wage increase.

Following page: Mailroom workers assembled newspapers by hand in the early 1950s.

suburban newspapers who chafed at what they characterized as *The Star's* attempts to deny them business. In 1980 a descendant of one of the small publishers recalled in an interview his father's visiting Truman to urge him on.

Based on testimony at the trial, the small publications had plenty to annoy them. Witness after witness — merchants, theater owners, a onetime ballplayer-turned-florist — told how *Star* ad salesmen pressured them to get out or stay out of even the smallest local paper. Emil Sees, head of advertising and indicted along with the newspaper, was described as demanding that his salesmen threaten any *Star* advertiser who also bought space in the *Independent*, which covered society news, or *The Call*, which served black readers, or *Prom*, a publication aimed at teenagers, or the *Prairie Scout*, a tiny newsletter published in Prairie Village in the heart of the brand-new Johnson County suburbs. Many small specialty newspapers and magazines sprang up around Kansas City after World War II.

Other witnesses complained that Sees and his salesmen had tried to keep their ads out of the *Kansas City Journal*, a daily metro competitor until it closed in 1942.

The advertisers were variously told to buy as much space in *The Star* as in the competing publication (prohibitive because of the vast difference in rates), or that their ads would be buried beneath other ads and toward the back pages of *The Star*.

Part of the government complaint stemmed from the company's practice of printing two editions a day. Since William Rockhill Nelson purchased the failing *Times* in 1901 and made it the morning version of the afternoon *Star*, the company had treated the two papers as one. Each covered 12 hours. When deadline for one publication passed, the other picked up the story without repeating information from the earlier edition.

Home-delivery subscribers were not allowed to take one or the other. A subscription brought *The Times* and *The Star* to the doorstep each weekday. Since the early 1900s, national and classified advertisers were required to purchase their ad in both. Like home-delivery subscribers, they were not allowed to pick morning or afternoon paper separately.

The government's argument was that those requirements helped shut out potential competing media from the market. *The Star's* circulation was so large and its reach so dominant that merchants had to advertise in it to prosper. Sometimes threatened with banishment if they advertised in other places, many merchants gave in.

The jury heard testimony of *Star* advertisers who tried it, anyway.

A retired dress shop owner, Tom Crawford, said he spent $1,500 on advertising in *The Star* in 1948, and about $500 in *The Kansas City Kansan* and the *Independent*. In autumn 1948, he began advertising in *Capper's Weekly*. Despite getting the bulk of his advertising dollar, *The Star* moved his ads to the bottom of the page or to the back

"...if you don't start behaving yourself, it's going to get a lot worse. You've got to quit wasting your money on other publications."

— Emil Sees, advertising director, quoted by Tom Crawford at antitrust trial, 1955

THE STAR & THE CITY

The jury that heard the evidence in The Star's *criminal trial took a little more than four hours to make its decision.*

of the paper, he said. So Crawford went to *The Star* to talk to advertising director Sees. "Well...Tom, if you don't start behaving yourself, it's going to get a lot worse," Crawford quoted Sees as saying. "You've got to quit wasting your money on other publications."

Former *Star* ad salesmen testified that Sees regularly scanned other publications and, upon seeing *Star* advertisers in them, demanded that the salesman either get the advertiser to buy equal space — at higher cost — in *The Star* or choose between *The Star* and the competitor.

The defense: Great results for advertisers

The allegations were met with *Star* denials: no advertisers were threatened; Star ad rates and subscription prices were among the lowest among all metro dailies; and the paper was the most effective advertising medium in the city. Was *The Star* being accused simply because of its success?

Indeed, the leaders of the paper followed the confident line laid down decades before by William Rockhill Nelson. In celebration of the paper's 50th anniversary in 1930, *The Star* quoted this conversation between Nelson and an "eastern newspaper friend:"

"You've got a pretty tight newspaper monopoly in Kansas City, haven't you,

colonel?"

"Perhaps so, but the only monopoly I recognize as legitimate is the monopoly of excellence. As long as we give people more for their money than they can buy anywhere else on earth, why shouldn't they take *The Star*?"

The trial began in January 1955 and was over by late February.

After deliberating barely more than four hours, the jury found *The Star* guilty of the criminal charges. Sees, they found, was guilty, too.

Upon exhausting its appeals of the criminal actions, the newspaper signed a consent decree with the government, settling a companion civil lawsuit. Without admitting guilt, the newspaper dropped its forced combination advertising rates, allowed subscribers to choose one of the daily newspapers, and sold its television and radio stations. That was done by late 1957.

The consent decree spawned lawsuits from small publishers across the metropolitan area, most of which were settled at a cost to the newspaper of almost $1 million.

A humbled *Star* emerged from the fracas.

"It was a sorry, expensive, frustrating and in some respects humiliating experience," Roberts wrote. The president of the newspaper, who entered the battle confident of victory, wound up devoting much of his energy to the trial, the appeals and the subsequent lawsuits. By the time of the consent decree Roberts was nearly 70 years old. He rued how the litigation "almost completely engrossed the time and attention of management" — a management of which he stood at the top.

The Star would live with the consent decree for four decades. And with its leadership distracted, *The Star* went on no great crusades.

Indeed, the testimony had laid bare strains with segments of its readership. Here were small businessmen, willing to go before a jury to tell how the paper's advertising department called the shots. Add to them the political foes of *The Star*'s regularly Republican leanings, and it was publicly obvious that the newspaper had built resentment among a least a considerable minority of Kansas Citians.

Into the big leagues

Though chastened by the decree and hesitant to embark on new crusades, *The Star* continued to be the dominant news and advertising medium in Kansas City. Readers still received an expansive, evolving newspaper that was selling copies and making money.

And if *The Star* 's news and editorial pages lost some of their thunder, rumbles now came from the sports department. Its editor, Ernie Mehl, wanted to turn Kansas City into something it had not been in the 20th century — a major-league city.

His inspiration came in the early 1950s, when the Boston Braves decided to

pull up stakes and move west to Milwaukee. It was the first move of a major-league baseball franchise since before the days of Babe Ruth. There were only 16 teams in those days, none west or south of St. Louis, and baseball was the country's dominant professional sport.

When he first heard of the Braves' move, Mehl was on the west coast of Florida covering spring training. Aboard a ferry carrying him from Bradenton to St. Petersburg, Mehl thought about how Milwaukee had built a stadium and how major-league baseball had come. Kansas City, he decided, needed to do something of the same.

At the official announcement of the Braves' change, Mehl wrote, he "positively drooled while listening to the Milwaukee writers discuss what they expected would happen there. And, we thought, the same thing could happen to Kansas City."

As his protégé, Joe McGuff, later recalled, Mehl set out on a personal campaign to bring baseball to Kansas City.

"Ernie was the one," McGuff said, "who really pushed the button."

Mehl, sports editor since 1950, worked the businessmen of Kansas City, trying to assemble enough people and money to bid for the St. Louis Browns. The Browns were a likely prospect, because they had to share the St. Louis market with the more successful and more popular Cardinals. Mehl enlisted Kansas City

With an upper deck added to attract major-league baseball, Municipal Stadium was packed for big games, such as when the New York Yankees came to town.

Mehl

Starbeams

Live in a house by the side of the road if you want to but don't try backing out of your driveway during a rush hour.

Tax cuts can be confusing, unless you remember the basic principle that they don't mean you will pay any less in taxes.

We're all in favor of saving the whale, a magnificent mammal with the additional advantage of never following the children home from school.

The Russians report that chocolate bars left at the North Pole in 1900 are still tasty. A couple which slipped behind the car seat last August were not so fortunate.

Since its first issue in 1880, *The Star* had carried a column of brief items called Starbeams. Their nature changed as their proprietor changed, although they were often short one- or two-sentence witticisms. In 1946, Starbeams was taken over by Bill Vaughan and he maintained it until he died in 1977. Through it, and through short essays published regularly in *The Star* and *The Times*, the "paragrapher" became the newspaper's most recognizable contributor. The Starbeams above are his.

He filled Starbeams with fictitious characters that proved immensely popular. By the end, he had written an estimated 100,000 Starbeam items – starring characters such as Senator Sludgepump, Cousin Fuseloyle, Tillie and the Loud Voice on the Bus.

Vaughan was regularly published in *Reader's Digest, Better Homes and Gardens* (under the pseudonym Burton Hillis) and in newspapers nationwide. In addition, he produced 3,500 full-length columns and political reporting from national conventions.

Over time, one Vaughan column stands out. The first known instance of its printing was on Christmas Day 1960. It was reprinted occasionally until 1981. Since then, it has appeared every year at Christmastime.

Pipe-smoking Bill Vaughan at his typewriter: a raconteur of the first order.

Vaughan's "The Best Christmas Story of Them All"

"Tell me a story of Christmas," she said.

The television mumbled faint inanities in the next room. From a few houses down the block came the sound of car doors slamming and guests being greeted with large cordiality.

Her father thought awhile. His mind went back over the interminable parade of Christmas books he had read at the bedside of his children.

"Well," he started, tentatively, "once upon a time, it was the week before Christmas, and all the little elves at the North Pole were sad."

"I'm tired of elves," she whispered. And he could tell she was tired, maybe almost as weary as he was himself after the last few feverish days.

"OK," he said. "There was once, in a city not very far from here, the cutest wriggly little puppy you ever saw. The snow was falling, and this little puppy didn't have a home. As he walked along the streets, he saw a house that looked quite a bit like our house. And at the window —"

"Was a little girl who looked quite a bit like me," she said with a sigh. "I'm tired of puppies. I love Pinky, of course. I mean story puppies."

"OK," he said. "No puppies. This narrows the field."

"What?"

"Nothing. I'll think of something. Oh, sure. There was a forest, way up in the North, farther even than where Uncle Ed lives. And all the trees were talking about how each one was going to be the grandest Christmas tree of all. One said, 'I am going to stand in front of the White House where the President of the whole United States lives, and everybody will see me.'

"And another beatutiful tree said, proudly, 'I am going to be in the middle of New York City and all the people will see me and think I am the most beautiful tree in the world.'

"And then a little fir tree spoke up and said, 'I am going to be a Christmas tree, too.' And all the trees laughed and laughed and said: 'A Christmas tree? You? Who would want you?' "

"No trees, Daddy," she said. "We have a tree at school and at Sunday school and at the supermarket and downstairs and a little one in my room. I am very tired of trees."

"You are very spoiled," he said.

"Hmmm," she replied. "Tell me a Christmas story."

"Let's see. All the reindeer up at the North Pole were looking forward to pulling Santa's sleigh. All but one, and he felt sad because," he began with a jolly ring in his voice but quickly realized that this wasn't going to work either.

His daughter didn't say anything; she just looked at him reproachfully.

"Tired of reindeer, too?" he asked. "Frankly, so am I. How about Christmas on the farm when I was a little boy? Would you like to hear about how it was in the olden days, when my grandfather would heat up bricks and put them in the sleigh and we'd all go for a ride?"

"Yes, Daddy," she said, obediently. "But not right now. Not tonight."

He was silent, thinking. His repertoire, he was afraid, was exhausted. She was quiet, too. Maybe, he thought, I'm home free.

Maybe she has gone to sleep.

"Daddy," she murmured. "Tell me a story of Christmas."

Then it was as though he could read the words, so firmly were they in his memory. Still holding her hand, he leaned back:

"And it came to pass in those days, that there went out a decree from Caesar Augustus, that all the world should be taxed..."

Her hand tightened a bit in his, and he told her a story of Christmas.

Mayor William Kemp and members of the City Council, heads of department stores and grocery chains. All gave time, energy and advice — but none had the money to buy a baseball franchise. Neither did Kansas City have a stadium big enough.

The financially troubled Browns did, indeed, pull up stakes. But they headed east instead of west, and in 1954 became the Baltimore Orioles.

Undaunted by Kansas City's weak efforts at financing — he recalled no more than $50,000 was pledged — Mehl began casting about for outside owners willing to support a team in Kansas City. Help came from a co-owner of the New York Yankees, Del Webb. Because the Yankees owned Kansas City's minor-league Blues, Mehl had struck up a friendship with Webb. Webb pointed to the Athletics in Philadelphia, where Connie Mack was growing old. Perhaps Mack and his family would be willing to sell the team.

In addition, Webb pointed Mehl toward a potential owner. He was Arnold Johnson, a Chicago real estate mogul and high official in the Automatic Canteen Company of America, which made vending machines. Johnson had recently invested in baseball, having bought Yankee Stadium and the 17,000-seat stadium used by the Yankee's top farm club, the Blues. He leased them back to Webb and the Yankees in a complex deal that helped them all reduce or avoid taxes.

Mehl's first entreaty was made when Johnson visited Kansas City for a meeting of Automatic Canteen Co. officials. Johnson wasn't interested.

"I have talked to enough baseball club owners," Mehl recalled Johnson's saying, "to know something about their headaches."

On a second occasion, Johnson turned Mehl down. And then on a third.

Persevering, Mehl stopped in Chicago in June 1954 on his way to Cleveland for the major league All-Star Game. By then, Kansas City had placed a bond issue on the Aug. 3 ballot to raise money to buy and refurbish the stadium at 22nd and Brooklyn. Mehl called Johnson.

"Where have you been all morning?" Johnson asked Mehl. "Why?"

"I'm going to try to buy the Athletics for Kansas City. You've sold me."

Behind the scenes at midcentury.
Clockwise from above left: A Linotype
operator set type in lead, one line at
a time. Want-ad takers wrote orders.
Stereotypers prepared plates for the
presses. Mailroom staffers assembled
and bundled newspapers.

Facing page: The newsroom was
furnished with oak desks and manual
typewriters in 1958.

Alvin S. McCoy, The Star's longtime Kansas correspondent, won a Pulitzer Prize in 1954 for exposing a kickback scheme involving the GOP National Chairman, a Kansan. Roy Roberts, a leading Republican, was embarrassed by the story and McCoy had to enter himself in the competition.

In September 1963, Attorney General Robert F. Kennedy Jr., visiting Kansas City to speak to the Missouri Bar, dropped by The Star. While there, he watched a Senate subcommittee's televised hearing into organized crime. He chatted with Roy Roberts, who had lost a considerable amount of weight by that time.

Noting the success of the Braves' move to Milwaukee, Johnson realized a million fans a year could make him some money. And when Johnson got interested, little could stop him, not even a syndicate of Philadelphians formed to try to keep the team in town. On Aug. 3, Kansas City's bond improvement program — which required a two-thirds majority — passed with more than 78 percent of the vote. The stadium would become Kansas City's. Now, it needed a team.

After on-and-off negotiations over several late summer and fall months, the day arrived that had been set by Mack for competing purchasers — Johnson and the Philadelphia group — to discuss things. This discussion would take place at Mack's apartment in Philadelphia.

Johnson stole a march, using an acquaintance with Mack's chauffeur to sneak into Mack's apartment early. Before leaving, Johnson had handed Mack a check for earnest money, the first installment on the $3 million the purchase would require, and the Athletics were his. Kansas City would be part of the major leagues.

On April 12, 1955, the Athletics played their first game in the stadium at 22nd and Brooklyn, now turned over to the city, expanded by proceeds of the bond issue and renamed Municipal Stadium. The city went nuts. Kansas City was one of the eight select cities listed each day in the American League standings.

As it turned out, the A's never ranked much above the bottom in those standings. As the 1950s wore on, Athletics fans noticed how Johnson's close ties with the Yankee owners led to continual trades of the A's top players to the Bronx. Yet although the A's of those days were no champs, their mere presence had put Kansas City in the national pantheon.

Mehl's negotiations took place away from the pages of the newspaper, but clearly his position on *The Star* and the newspaper's standing in the city gave him the entrée he needed. As for *The Star*, A's coverage was put in the hands of a 28-year-old Oklahoma native who had been covering the Kansas City Blues — Joe McGuff. Over the next dozen years, he would ride a baseball rollercoaster that would stop only when baseball was preserved for Kansas City.

The city is its apple

Although its crusading fires were banked in the 1950s, *The Star* still supported most civic improvements, endorsing bond issues like the one for the stadium in front-page editorials.

Where the newspaper excelled was its exhaustive coverage of local news. The Pulitzer-winning effort for the 1951 flood was an example. Coverage of the kidnaping and murder of Bobby Greenlease, son of a wealthy Cadillac dealer, was another. The Ruskin Heights tornado of 1957 tore up mile after mile of homes and businesses south of the city limits, many of the neighborhoods newly developed, and took more than 40 lives. In 1959, a petroleum tank exploded on Southwest Boulevard at State line, killing four firefighters and a volunteer. For those big stories and for scores of others, in words and in pictures *The Star* and *The Times* printed impressively detailed, insightful and thorough coverage.

In 1963, in his mid-70s and slowed by cataracts and ulcers, Roberts gave up the president's chair and became chairman of the board. He was succeeded by Richard Fowler. Like Roberts, Fowler was a product of *The Star*'s newsroom, but unlike Roberts he was a quiet, introspective man, formerly head of the editorial page and co-author of *City of The Future* 13 years before. Fowler emphasized good writing and demanded longer, more analytical stories from his news staff.

The Star sent a reporter to the South for 14 weeks to examine the civil rights revolution there. Another reporter was dispatched to Vietnam.

Under Fowler, the newspaper turned in a more thoughtful direction. Arts coverage was boosted on Sundays and a Sunday analysis section created. Special sections looked at world issues.

Through the 1960s, *The Star* supported local efforts at civic betterment, although its work was nothing like the all-out, one-sided crusades of Nelson's day. It backed the bond issues for establishing the Truman Sports Complex, and supported the building of a new airport. As Kansas City constructed new public super-buildings, *The Star* was there to approve.

Inside *The Star* building Fowler oversaw installation of new, automated equipment for typesetting and photocomposition. In 1966, *The Star* purchased new Hoe presses. They were the last new presses to be placed in the brick building at 18th and Grand.

For *The Star* as a business concern, Fowler worried that it was reaching its limit. In the 1960s, inflation constantly pushed up costs and wages followed along. If that kept on, Fowler worried, profits would eventually diminish. He urged his fellow board members to diversify the company and soon.

In a sense, *The Star* had been diversified since the late 1940s, when it purchased a Wisconsin paper mill. The newsprint restrictions of World War II forced *The Star* to turn away advertisers, limit news coverage and even turn down subscribers. To avoid those consequences, which were awful for the paper's balance sheet, the company sought a ready source and found it in the Flambeau Paper Co. of Park Falls, Wis. Through 1949, Flambeau kept *The Star* supplied with newsprint, and then when the newsprint crunch eased, it turned to making high-grade papers. Meanwhile, *The Star* invested about $1 million in an Alabama newsprint mill, a joint arrangement with papers in St. Louis and Cleveland. Additionally, it made new contracts with Canadian suppliers.

In 1965, at Fowler's urging, *The Star* paid $4.9 million for a color printing plant in suburban Chicago called Cadillac Printing and Lithographing Corp. It served the booming textbook business and printed in-flight airline magazines. Some editors hoped it would print a revived Sunday magazine for *The Star*. In 1966, *The Star* bought the *Great Bend Tribune* in central Kansas, and in 1968 The *Colorado*

May 21, 1957, the morning after the Ruskin Heights tornado, this was the account.

Fowler

Growth in the suburbs led to the establishment of outlying offices for The Star. *this was the Johnson County office at Johnson Drive and Nall.*

In 1966 The Star ordered the last presses it would ever install at 18th and Grand. They were all up and running by 1968.

Transcript in Golden.

Socially and physically, the city changes

Through those years, Kansas City was on the move, although the direction was not always clear. The airport, hemmed in by the Missouri River, was clearly inadequate. The city's major-league franchise, the A's, now had an owner who threatened over and over to pick up and leave. Crowds watching the new professional football team, the Chiefs, were bursting the seams of old Municipal Stadium. By the end of the decade, those would be addressed by massive building projects that created Kansas City International Airport and the Truman Sports Complex.

The newspaper market was changing, too. The metropolitan area continued its march away from downtown. *The Star* began publishing weekly zoned sections, tailored for various parts of Greater Kansas City. Meanwhile, readers were forming new habits. In 1965 circulation of the morning *Times* reached 347,742, exceeding for the first time *The Star's*. More and more, subscribers wanted their paper in the morning, and that represented the stirrings of a lifestyle change that would gain momentum and threaten the afternoon paper in Kansas City and in metro areas across the country.

More difficult to address, for *The Star* and its city, was the matter of race. Although the paper had never displayed virulent racism, it had adopted an attitude common to many people of the Middle West — that black people could be largely ignored. In the pages of the newspaper, black people were identified as Negroes at least as late as 1961. Few pictures of black people ran in the paper and reports of

In April 1968, after the assassination of Martin Luther King Jr., civil rights marchers carried signs through downtown Kansas City, Kan. There, schools were let out the day of King's funeral. In Kansas City, schools were kept in session and protests eventually turned violent. For five nights looting, burning and shooting scarred Kansas City's East side.

civil rights demonstrations were played with caution.

The national civil rights revolution, however, foreshadowed change. So did surveys the newspaper conducted of its black readers. By 1963, they found, about 40 percent of black-owned households subscribed to *The Star*.

Fowler acted. Most racial identifications were eliminated from articles, and stories about black achievements were promoted. In 1963, the newsroom employed its first black person. One by one came black reporters and copy editors. As the paper struggled to make its staff correspond to the city it covered, the city continued to fester in racial matters. In April 1968, riots broke out in the wake of Martin Luther King's funeral — a wakeup call to white people throughout the metropolitan area. That September, *The Star* published an unprecedented 20-page special section on race relations in Kansas City.

The Star's relationship with the black community had its ups and downs over the years afterward, but the newspaper had shown it could at least begin to move beyond its past ignoring and downgrading of black people.

What the newspaper had difficulty moving beyond were the challenges coming from within. Fowler stepped down as president in autumn 1968.

His successor, Paul Miner, inherited a difficult financial situation. The Cadillac investment had gone sour almost as soon as it was completed. Cadillac's books were not studied carefully before the purchase, and various liabilities cropped up. Textbook purchases dropped, as did the airline business. Cadillac's internal controls were slipshod and management lax. Productivity suffered. In the last quarter of 1968, Cadillac was kept afloat by money from *The Star*. No taker was

Miner

The Chiefs won the Super Bowl in 1970, when they played their regular season games in Municipal Stadium. By 1972 they had moved into their new home, Arrowhead Stadium, one of two at the Harry S. Truman Sports Complex in eastern Kansas City.

found until 1973. By then, *The Star* had taken a $3 million bath on the deal.

In 1972, *The Star* sold the Great Bend paper at a profit, and in 1975 it sold the Colorado paper, which was only breaking even. When Miner arrived in the head job, he had little chance to ponder how to make Kansas City better. He was too busy trying to save *The Star*.

Once again, a sports editor weighed in for the paper and the city.

After Arnold Johnson died unexpectedly in 1960, another Chicagoan, Charles O. Finley, bought the A's. Although Finley tried varous publicity stunts at Municipal Stadium, some outrageous and some prescient, attendance in Kansas City never suited him, and Finley began issuing open threats to move the team out of town. In October 1967, only 12 years after they arrived, the A's packed up and moved to Oakland, Calif.

Joe McGuff, the paper's top baseball writer, suffered through Finley's tenure and now led a spirited charge to get a new franchise and find a new owner. He and Mehl went to the major league baseball meetings that took place right after the A's departure. Owners told them Kansas City would get a new team "sometime after the next two years."

Unsatisfied by the vague reply, the two Kansas Citians pulled aside Red Sox owner Tom Yawkey, begging him to persuade his fellow owners to promise Kansas City a team no later than 1969. Yawkey, seeing their passion, gathered several owners for dinner. Along with them went Sen. Stuart Symington, as good an indicator as any of the seriousness with which Kansas City approached the quest.

Baseball approved. Kansas City would get its team in time for the 1969 season.

Meanwhile, Mehl and his childhood neighbor, Earl Smith, worked on Ewing Kauffman, who headed Marion Laboratories, a Kansas City pharmaceuticals firm. Kauffman was worth $104 million, *Fortune* magazine said, but was reluctant to take the plunge. Mehl and Smith were quick to remind Kauffman how, despite his wealth, no one in Kansas City really knew him. Kauffman's mind began to change and with a little more persuasion, he pledged to put up the $10 million to buy the new team. It would begin play at Municipal Stadium as the Kansas City Royals, then move to the new Truman Sports Complex.

Kauffman

The Star gets an offer

Things continued more unhappily than not within the newspaper company.

While worries about the paper's outside investments consumed Miner and the board, staff concerns sprouted. In 1970 and 1972, newsroom staff tried to organize a guild, but failed. Union pressmen went on strike in 1974, but were fired and their contract canceled. Production technology, meanwhile, outpaced *The Star*'s resources and its ability to handle the transition from hot lead to electronic publishing. Many days, the paper simply looked haggard.

Miner, too, often looked haggard, burdened like the rest of the board with problems that had come in an avalanche and that extended beyond their experience. Fearing for his health, Miner stepped down in January 1975. Two days later, he suffered a heart attack.

That ushered in the last person to hold the title as president of *The Star* under employee ownership. He was W.W. Baker, once a reporter, then an editorial writer and later editor of the editorial page.

What might once have seemed a plum job was now simply a difficult one. The Flambeau paper mill was charged with polluting downstream from its plant, and the Environmental Proction Agency ordered installation of about $12 million of anti-pollution equipment. Graham paper, purchased only a few years before, made money but not enough to help the entire operation's bottom line. Meanwhile, federal law required the company to spend about $4 million to buy back shares from its pension trust. *Star* stock was not selling the way it once did to employees.

On Oct. 8, 1976, Baker received a phone call from the holding company that owned E.F. Hutton. For $120 million — all cash with no strings — a company called Capital Cities Communications was willing to buy *The Star*. It would take on the subsidiaries, too, failing or otherwise. Other offers came but none matched that.

The Star *changes hands: Directors met with Capital Cities representatives to turn over the company in February 1977 at a law office Downtown. Capital Cities officer Thomas Murphy, above, consoled Star President W. W. Baker.*

The Star had its own assessment, which valued it at $88.3 million. The Capital Cities offer, eventually raised to $125 million, was too good to pass up. Capital Cities Communications knew of *The Star's* economic woes, yet the New Yorkers saw possibilities with the right management moves. After all, Kansas City was still a one-newspaper market.

Soon, the possibility of a sale to an outside company became widely known.

Inside *The Star*, there was much concern, and it was shared by many in the city. Since Nelson and Morss published their first issue in 1880, *The Star* had been locally owned. Since Irwin Kirkwood assembled the staff bid in 1926, the newspaper had been owned by its own employees and retirees.

As the possibility of a sale moved toward probability, every employee from President Baker on down knew an era was ending before their eyes.

On Feb. 15, 1977, before winter had ended, the deal was done. *The Star's* management would report to New York City.

Changing times: *Star* ads of the 1950s and 1970s

1955

1976

1976 - 2006

A   RISING   STAR

I n September 1980, *The Star* turned 100 years old and threw a big party for itself.

Hundreds of civic leaders gathered for a banquet at the Radisson Muehlebach Hotel, where Vice President Walter Mondale was the featured speaker. A 192-page commemorative centennial section accompanied the Sunday paper to every subscriber's doorstep. That section was converted into a handsome, oversized book and every employee got a copy. Star Co. workers were treated to a lavish reception at the Alameda Plaza, where they dined on mounds of boiled shrimp and other treats from a massive buffet.

As those weeklong festivities began, the company announced it would give $1 million to the Nelson Gallery.

"*The Star* and the gallery have long been synonymous," said President and Publisher James H. Hale, "both the product of Nelson's aspirations."

The celebration of the newspaper's first century vividly reminded readers — and not coincidentally the paper's employees — of *The Star*'s role in the city it served.

The Star in 1980 was the central marketplace for ideas and information in Kansas City. Its readership far outnumbered the viewership of any local television station — and rivaled the viewership of all the stations combined. No other information source challenged its dominance.

Certainly, the newspaper still stirred as much anger as acclaim. Surely, neither its staff nor its management nor its contents were as diverse as the metropolitan area. Yet *The Star* was ubiquitous. In its pages, rich and middle-class and poor, young and old, liberal and moderate and conservative discovered what the rest of the city was up to.

1976

Population	
Kansas City, Mo.	477,000
Seven-county total	1,340,000
Average number of pages	90*
Average circulation	315,248

* Times and Star total

Facing page: Publisher James H. Hale exulted when the Pulitzer prizes were announced in 1982.

THE KANSAS CITY STAR.

THE FIRST
100 YEARS

A man, a newspaper and a city

The early 1980s saw The Star *mark its centennial, above, and win two Pulitzer prizes.*

Davies

Certainly, the paper did not decide the course of events — although it freely issued its opinions. What friends and foes alike acknowledged was that its reporting and editorializing set the agenda for Kansas City's debates. *The Star* started people talking.

That close relationship — newspaper and city — thrived even though the company that paid for all centennial banquets and the commemorative publications was situated in New York City.

A new attitude, a new look

In 1926, when the Nelson estate trustees were selling *The Star* to the highest bidder, staff members and people in the community fretted about the threat of outside ownership. Fifty years later, when outside ownership arrived, the same worries arose. Yet the deal with Capital Cities strengthened *The Star* and its voice.

The Star's old board-of-directors form of governance, local though it was, grew cautious through the years. Leadership by committee required consensus, and consensus became difficult to achieve. Slumping profits affected the entire organization. Equipment and staff morale showed it. News coverage diminished in quantity and in quality, and production values dropped, too.

The new owners were dedicated to profit the way the employee ownership had not been. And they plowed some of those new profits back into the product. *The Star* built muscle as it prepared for the technological and social change that came rapidly in the 1970s and 1980s.

After taking over in 1977, Capital Cities promptly set to work. It installed its own publisher, James H. Hale, a lifelong newspaperman. Hale arrived from Fort Worth, where he had run Capital Cities' *Star-Telegram.*

Like William Rockhill Nelson, Hale tried to avoided large public settings. Like Nelson, he was direct and decisive in private. Hale was a consummate newspaper businessman, too, and made Capital Cities' investment pay off surprisingly fast.

Within months Hale hired his own division heads — new leaders for advertising, production, circulation and news. They trimmed people and spending throughout the company, overhauled tables of organization, tightened accounting and cranked up revenues. In every area, waste came under a microscope. Once the dust settled, the economic health of the company improved. Gradually, it became clear to employees that the health of the product would improve along with it. After Hale's initial rounds of cuts, spending grew. Salaries and staffing increased. With profits rising, *The Star* opened more news bureaus, added staff and upgraded computer equipment in every department.

As editor, the newspaper's second-most visible position, Hale hired Michael J. Davies from *The Courier-Journal* in Louisville, Ky. Davies was the first top editor hired from outside the company since the 19th century.

Under employee ownership, division leaders had put in long years of service and had risen through the ranks. Davies, only in his 30s when he started work, had never worked a day at *The Star*.

Davies' charge from Hale was to reinvigorate news coverage. Hale turned the editorial pages over to James Scott, a veteran of the newspaper. Hale got what he asked from Davies and Scott. The paper strengthened its editorial stands and aggressively pursued news.

Davies turned on its head the nearly 80-year-old system under which the morning *Times* and the afternoon *Star* acted as cooperating newspapers, each covering separate 12-hour segments of the day. Already, Hale had removed the line above *The Times* nameplate that said, "(The Morning *Kansas City Star*)." Readers were showing a preference for morning delivery. Besides, the afternoon paper's delivery was growing more difficult as the metro area expanded outward. Afternoon outstate circulation plummeted.

Retooled Star *and* Times *no longer looked or acted like twins.*

For more and more readers, the morning *Times* was the only paper they received. Under Davies' plan, *The Times* was to pursue regional and national stories without ignoring Kansas City, and *The Star* was to become intensely local. Where reporting beats overlapped — as they did at City Hall, the state capitals and the courts — the papers were to compete.

Like Davies, the idea was imported from Louisville. Nevertheless, the separate roles roughly matched each newspaper's circulation pattern. Competition naturally made the two papers livelier and more responsive, although news sources accustomed to the old arrangement were dismayed when they found reporters from the same company battling one another for the same information.

The contents of the two papers were reorganized and standardized into regular sections for national and international news , local news, features and sports. Each paper was redesigned with its own distinctive typeface and overall appearance.

To give the two papers a human face, columns were instituted, bearing logos with their authors' pictures. Previously, sports editors, some arts and entertainment writers and occasional editorial staffers had standing columns, but rarely with their photograph. Bill Vaughan's humor column had appeared for years on the front page of each paper once a week, accompanied by a sketch of him. For many, Vaughan had been the paper's human face, but he died in early 1977.

Now *The Times* handed Arthur S. Brisbane a column on the front page of its new Metropolitan section and *The Star* gave a regular column to Charles W. Gusewelle.

Brisbane   *Gusewelle*

Heaster   *McGuff*

Inside the lobby of the Hyatt Regency on the day after the skywalks collapsed, heavy equipment picked through the wreckage. Survivors were comforted by others outside the hotel, left, and employees consoled one another, below.

The Times instituted a sports section column opposite Joe McGuff's longstanding column in *The Star*. *The Star* hired a new business editor, Jerry Heaster, who wrote a regular column. Investigative and enterprise reporting — the kind that delved deeper into events and trends — was encouraged.

Once placed on solid economic footing, *The Star* and *Times* gave Kansas City more and timelier news coverage, better presented.

Two events symbolized the change.

A sudden disaster. A long decline

One event was quick and castrophic. It occurred on a Friday night in July 1981, as couples danced to big-band music in the lobby of the newly opened Hyatt Regency hotel in the Crown Center complex. Suddenly the building's architectural signature — its suspended skywalks — crashed to the lobby floor. More than 100 persons died, crushed by the weight of the skywalks or suffocated in the dust and rubble. Nearly 200 more were injured.

The Star and *Times* deployed reporters, photographers and graphic artists to cover the disaster in minute detail. Using outside experts and dogged reporting by its own staff, *The Star* uncovered the engineering design flaw that led to the catastrophe. Even in the face of pressure from some Kansas Citians to restrain their coverage, the papers persevered in digging for the truth. For their work on the skywalks collapse, *The Star* and *Times* won the 1982 Pulitzer prize for local general or spot news reporting. The same year, *Times* reporter Rick Atkinson won a Pulitzer for national reporting.

The other event was years in the making. Kansas City was falling behind comparable cities around the country. *The Star* set out to discover why and to find a solution. *Star* reporters and photographers visited 17 cities and interviewed more than 200 business, community and government leaders in those places and in Kansas City.

Kansas City, they found, had become the Fort Wayne, Indiana, of a century earlier — the one from which William Rockhill Nelson and Samuel Morss departed for greener pastures. The metropolitan area was stagnating at the very moment other cities were charging forward.

In Kansas City of the 1980s, *The Star* found leadership in disarray. The multitude of metro area jurisdictions — more than 100 cities, several counties, two states — formed a mass of squabbling competitors. The central city schools were in shambles, the job market was tight, infrastructure was crumbling and Downtown dying.

The result of the study was a weeklong series of articles published in June 1983 and labeled "Blueprint for Progress." The series reported how other cities had gained momentum through dynamic leadership, community consensus and a well-supported plan for growth.

The Times, July 18, 1981. The toll would rise.

Rick Atkinson covered national matters for The Times in the early 1980s and won a Pulitzer in 1982 for his work.

The 1980s saw Kansas City's Downtown take on a new look with big new hotels and skyscrapers.

Harking back to methods much employed by *The Star* under William Rockhill Nelson, the "Blueprint for Progress" articles took a decidedly pro-growth tone. On its front page *The Star* noted that the series departed from the 1980s norm of mainstream journalism, which held that news columns ought to refrain from advocacy. "Blueprint" made suggestions and issued challenges, nudging the boundaries. Some reporters and editors had dissented, *The Star* wrote, but "the topic was of such importance and the choices so clear that it should be done."

"Blueprint" was right down Nelson's and Morss' alley.

Growing upward — but also outward

The reinvigorated *Star* and *Times* got noticed, for good or ill. Indeed, many civic leaders complained about what they called the newspaper's growing negative bent. That feeling climaxed in the newspapers' coverage of the Hyatt collapse. In Kansas City, many sympathized with the hotel property's owner, Hallmark Cards Inc., considered the city's leading corporate citizen.

The Star sought responses to its "Blueprint for Progress" series from many of those same leaders and got them, stretching for weeks after the initial articles. Some viewed "Blueprint" as negative because it pointed to greater successes in other cities. Many, however, saw it as a call to arms.

The series became, as the editors hoped, a forum for Kansas Citians to consider the problems of local leadership and local turf battles.

Even as the series was going to press, new skyscrapers were in the works, chief among them the Vista hotel at 11th and Wyandotte streets. After the Vista came new housing on nearby Quality Hill. Then came the AT&T Town Pavilion at 12th and Main streets. As the 1980s wore on came construction of One Kansas City Place and other skyscrapers inside the Downtown freeway loop. That constituted the biggest building boom Downtown since the 1920s, and the Kansas City skyline took on a distinctly more modern appearance.

Downtown's problems weren't solved — nor those of the metropolitan area — but "Blueprint" had synthesized them and brought them to Kansas City's attention. *The Star* had put the matter on the public agenda.

Even as Downtown reached upward in the 1980s, the Kansas City metropolitan area kept sprawling outward. Subdivision after subdivision gobbled up farmland to the southwest in Johnson County and to the southeast in Jackson County. These new residential neighborhoods featured ever larger houses and larger yards, nearby shopping malls and school districts with good reputations. Homeowners flocked to them.

The older parts of the city of Kansas City, Missouri, proper — neighborhoods south of the Missouri River and inside the pre-war boundaries of the city — kept losing population. Like a cell, Kansas City kept dividing.

Since the 1970s, the afternoon *Star* had published zoned editions with articles and advertising aimed for different sections of town. Now in the 1980s, *The Star* expanded that effort, moving from four separate zoned sections to seven and more. Late in the decade, the morning *Times* split its daily paper into an edition covering Johnson County and one covering the rest of the metropolitan area

More colorful, finer-tuned

In 1986, a Star veteran once again assumed the editor's chair. Joe McGuff, longtime sports editor and columnist, took over the newsroom. It would be his last assignment before retirement. Much respected around Kansas City inside and outside the world of sports, McGuff had developed a reputation as a fair man with patient, measured judgment. Having watched able reporters and editors come and go through the 1980s, he strove to make *The Star* and *Times* even more part of their community, insisting on hiring midwesterners when possible in hopes they would commit themselves to the paper for the long term.

McGuff had once asked a group of children what they wanted to see in a newspapers. "Color!" they replied. Knowing that technology now permitted more and better-reproduced color, McGuff demanded color photographs every day on the front page of each paper.

Sadly, McGuff also had to preside over the demise of one of the papers. In the late 1980s, as the afternoon *Star*'s circulation and advertising diminished, the inevitable became all too obvious. Most large American cities already had lost their afternoon papers and now it was Kansas City's turn.

Declining circulation of the afternoon Star, *along with the costs of producing and distributing it, led to its death in early 1990. On March 1, a new edition combining the contents of* The Star *and* The Times *was issued under* The Star's *nameplate.*

A Star *investigative team toasted the newspaper's eighth Pulitzer prize, awarded in 1992 for a series of articles on the U.S. Department of Agriculture.*

Woodworth

On March 1, 1990, the staffs of *The Star* and *The Times* merged and instituted a combined morning newspaper named *The Kansas City Star*. For the first time since 1901, when Nelson bought *The Times*, the company was back to one newspaper a day. For the first time since founding of *The Kansas City Evening Star* in 1880, the company published no newspaper in the afternoon.

Within a few years of the combination, *The Star* instituted more than a dozen weekly tabloid-sized editions targeted to different parts of town. These little papers, each eventually named Neighborhood News for the area it covered, published "little" news, details of school activities and student honors, high school and lower-level sports, block-by-block crime logs, baby pictures and pages of readers' own snapshots. Everything was aimed at localizing *The Star*'s content. The sections appeared every Wednesday. In Johnson County and southern parts of the Missouri side of the metro area, the sections also appeared Saturdays. They were important additions to the news coverage and to advertising revenue. Financially, they were a clear success.

They helped alleviate the problem of having to cover in detail a vast, differentiated and in some parts fractured metropolitan area — a problem Nelson and Morss had not faced with they began their fiercely local *Star*.

In Hale's 15 years at the helm of the company, from 1977 to 1992, the papers accomplished much. Besides expanding staff, brightening its appearance, vastly improving its apperance and most years scoring record profits, it also won three Pulitzer prizes. *The Star*'s eighth Pulitzer — awarded for a 1991 investigation of the U.S. Department of Agriculture — came in McGuff's final months as editor.

Hale was succeeded by a young Capital Cities star, Robert C. Woodworth, and McGuff was succeeded by Arthur S. Brisbane, the popular *Times* columnist of the 1980s who after a stint at *The Washington Post* returned as columnist in 1990.

Under Brisbane's leadership of the newsroom, *The Star* once again sallied forth in the spirit of Nelson, waging local crusades. In the 20th century's last decade, however, the topics differed from those of Nelson's day. *The Star*'s longest crusade of the 1990s was waged on behalf of Kansas City's young people.

On Christmas Day, 1994, *The Star* told its readers that it would spend 1995 exploring the values that would guide the next generation. Week after week, month after month, and value by value, "Raising Kansas City" dived into issues chosen by a special panel of community members — and by surveys of teenagers. The idea, the paper said, was not to preach but to provide a place where parents could learn about matters they should discuss with their children. Along the way, every reader could explore the difficulties of morality in the modern era. Kansas City, after all, lay in the heart of a country despairing over a decline in morality. "Raising Kansas City" asked, What is right? How should one act?

Through 1995, fifty reporters, editors, photographers and graphic artists investigated the values listed by its panel and its survey respondents. The first

Far and away: This was Kansas City by the 1990s — office parks and subdivisions sprawling miles from Downtown.

was courage and what it means. Second was knowing right from wrong, and the importance of family in helping young people figure which was which. Compassion and kind acts were examined, along with awe and wonder — awe at human and natural greatness, wonder at how things became the way they are.

"Raising Kansas City" considered tenacity and its related values, persistence and commitment. Boundaries and limits came next, along with when to know when to stay within boundaries and when to test limits. Later, the paper examined the need for respect for others, and for justice and fairness. Then came love of learning and reverence for wisdom, along with tolerance and acceptance, and altruism and generosity and the proper use of money. Finally, the series explored honesty and integrity. The articles numbered 200 over the course of the year.

Brisbane summed up the series this way in December 1995, "Raising Kansas

City...has been about one basic idea: that it's time we put our children ahead of ourselves."

He acknowledged that "no newspaper article is powerful enough to change the way a community thinks about its children."

"Fortunately, here in the waning years of the 20th century, a great many Kansas Citians have come to believe we must invest more in our children," he wrote. "*The Star* undertook the Raising Kansas City project to add power and clarity to this movement."

Readers, he said, donated more than $20,000 to community causes highlighted in the articles. Ten truckloads of clothing were delivered to single mothers struggling to make it in the workplace. Three thousand people turned out for various community events that stemmed from the "Raising Kansas City" project, and nearly a thousand people joined mentoring and pen-pal programs. For the series, the newspaper won the first James K. Batten Award for Excellence in Civic Journalism. In 1996 the series turned to encouraging youth to participate in the democratic process and in 1997 moved to the Internet to build a series of local history websites.

While "Raising Kansas City" touched the large problem of youth, other *Star* writers took on the massive question of suburban sprawl. Kansas City, they found, was "America's shrine to sprawl." Over the last three decades, the urban and suburban land mass had doubled while the population had grown by less than one-third. Not only were Kansas Citians moving toward the edges, but they were consuming more space in doing so.

As suburban growth stretched the city away from its core, the fast-paced, wheel-and-deal U.S. economy of the 1990s rocked *The Star*.

New owners and new technologies

Since buying the Star Co. in 1977, Capital Cities Communications had expanded exponentially. In the mid-1980s, it acquired ABC, bringing into its fold a television network, a sports cable network and several big-city TV stations. Now, it was Capital Cities/ABC.

By the middle 1990s, that mixture attracted even bigger media companies. In March 1996 the Walt Disney Co. bought Capital Cities for its entertainment components. *The Star* and other newspapers didn't fit the Disney profile, so in 1997 they were put up for sale. Several suitors came looking, and the winning bid was offered by Knight Ridder, the second-largest newspaper company in the United States.

Itself the combination of two newspaper groups in the mid-1970s, Knight Ridder owned dozens of newspapers. In the newspaper industry, the company had a formidable reputation for the quality of its journalism and its working conditions. *The Star* was a good fit.

Brisbane

Amid the whirl of buying and selling, Woodworth left *The Star* and was succeeded as president and publisher by Brisbane. Now, the newspaper was under command of a veteran of the company. In turn Brisbane named as editor and vice-president native Kansas Citian Mark Zieman. *The Star* marched on.

For decades, changes in technology and in its readership kept *The Star* on the lookout for new ways to deliver information. In the 1990s *The Star* took its first major steps beyond the world of the daily newspaper since selling its radio and television properties in the '50s.

First came StarTouch, an interactive telephone service. Then experiments with a closed computer system led in the mid-1990s to establishment of a fledgling site on the World Wide Web, **KansasCity.com**. Since then, **KansasCity.com** has grown in use, in readership and in revenue — becoming a key element in *The Star*'s news operation.

Steadily, the newsroom retooled to serve not only the traditional morning print newspaper audience, but also the 24-hour hunger for breaking news on the Web. Also, **KansasCity.com** developed blogs and other features all its own to accompany

Campaigning for passage of a bistate sales tax, proponents of Science City and a renovated Union Station staged family events in autumn 1996. In November, voters in four counties approved the bistate tax.

The Star's *ever-evolving web page*

Star *President and Publisher Brisbane signed the papers committing the newspaper to construction of its new press and distribution plant Downtown.*

Charitable works: Over the years The Star *has helped establish several long-running Kansas City charities and supported many others. Since 1982 Project Warmth, above, has raised more than $7 million in contributions. The Coda Jazz Fund, below, was established in 2002 to help pay funeral and burial expenses for Kansas City jazz musicians.*

selected features from the daily newspaper. Its balance sheet, meanwhile, has moved into the black. After a decade's existence, **KansasCity.com** established itself as a primary Internet portal for news, sports and other information about Kansas City.

In the late 1990s, the newspaper entered a new publishing world with Kansas City Star Books, which produced volumes about local history, specialty books and a series of books on *Star* quilt patterns. Sports, business and political reporters found new outlets in Kansas City commercial and public radio, some with their own shows, others with regular appearances.

Its money where its words are

The building boom of the 1980s having long subsided, Kansas City's Downtown by the end of the 20th century was hurting. Despite a few encouraging changes such as growth in upper-end loft apartments, Downtown was littled lived in and increasingly little worked in. When *The Star* put Downtown under a microscope in autumn 2002, it found the area still a nowheresville. What to do? *The Star*, under Zieman's direction, took on the project in a series of articles, "Mending Our Broken Heart."

"Over the decades, city and civic leaders have devised plan after plan to save downtown Kansas City," the paper said. "But it's still bleak and boring."

Holding that a healthy downtown made a healthier metro area — and vice versa — the series found taxable private property values Downtown dropping. Residential population had bottomed out at barely 6,000.

Yet there were glimmers of hope — the re-opening of Union Station, development of the Crossroads arts district south of the freeway loop, and the developments by DST on the western edge of the freeway loop of Downtown. Some civic leaders who said it was the perfect time to begin recovering.

By the time the series ran, *The Star* was putting its money where its words were.

In 2002, Brisbane announced that Knight Ridder had given the go-ahead to build a new plant for *The Star*'s printing and distribution operations. No owner of *The Star* since the middle 1960s had bought new presses, always preferring to retool the old ones. No owner in *Star* history had constructed a separate building to house production facilities. Configuration of modern presses, however, would demand that.

Having considered sites near and far — in older areas and in the outer suburbs — Knight Ridder and its president, Tony Ridder, encouraged *The Star* to build its new $199 million press and packaging facility next door to its longtime headquarters. It would fill two city blocks from Truman Road to 17th Street and from Oak to McGee streets. That placed the structure just northeast of *The Star*'s old building. It would overlook the south end of the Downtown freeway loop.

"We have had a long-term presence Downtown," Brisbane said, "and we believe in the importance of Downtown and the future of Downtown. By constructing this adjacent to our current building, we think we get the best of both worlds."

The Star, he said, had taken on "considerable extra costs" to redevelop the Downtown site rather than to put its presses and hundreds of production employees in Lenexa, Olathe, Lee's Summit or Kansas City's East Side — all of which were considered.

In addition, the building would be more than a box for machinery. Architect Juan Moreno drew up a copper-and-glass structure with a main roof sloping up to the north, giving the appearance of making the leap over the interstate toward the

Before The Star's *project began, the land designated for it held parking lots, warehouses and small businesses. Two full blocks would be razed northeast of* Star *headquarters, which is at lower left.*

The new KBA presses

Tully

downtown skyline.

Ground was broken in spring 2003. By 2006, the structure was complete and printing of *The Star* began. State-of-the-art presses inside the building print color images on far more pages than *The Star*'s previous machinery. In addition, text and images print more crisply and in richer colors. Packaging machinery enhances precise distribution of zoned additions and of advertising. As a result of its new tools, in the early years of the 21st century *The Star* is printed and distributed with 21st-century methods.

The structure, named the Press Pavilion, was the first commitment to the new southern edge of Downtown to be transformed into steel and concrete. Since then, the elliptical, glass-covered H&R Block building has risen, the President Hotel has been remodeled, an entertainment district has broken ground, and a new Performing Arts Center has been promised. Largest of all, a new arena was rising across the interstate highway from the Press Pavilion. All created hope for Downtown's recovery.

Amid *The Star*'s massive physical change came more changes in management and ownership. In 2004 Knight Ridder elevated Brisbane to a corporate vice presidency and Mac Tully, a veteran of Capital Cities and Knight Ridder who spent several years early in his career at the Kansas City Star Co., was appointed publisher.

In 2005 three investor groups, unhappy with Knight Ridder's performance on the New York Stock Exchange, demanded the company act to improve their investments. Knight Ridder put itself up for sale. In early 2006 the company announced that it would be bought by McClatchy Newspapers Inc. McClatchy, headquartered at the 158-year-old *Bee* in Sacramento, Calif., then said it would sell a dozen of Knight Ridder's 32 papers and keep the rest. *The Kansas City Star*, it said, was a keeper.

As always with the newspaper, the single constant is change.

More than a century and a quarter has passed since *The Star* — in the language of the day — was "launched on the sea of Kansas City journalism." From its tiny second-floor headquarters on Delaware Street, to other homes rented and owned, to the big brick building at 18th and Grand constructed by William Rockhill Nelson, the paper has grown stride for stride with the city around it.

Sometimes comfortable with each other — and occasionally uneasy — *The Star* and the city have proved inseparable. For 125 years and more, they've been a match.

Its massive size lightened by glass walls, the Press Pavilion lets passersby see The Star's presses in operation. Behind the glass, copper and concrete are vast spaces for machinery to produce and package the newspaper.

Month by month, the site of the Press Pavilion was transformed. Right: These photographs, taken from the same spot atop The Star's headquarters building, document the change in the neighborhood beginning in October 2002, upper left. By July 2005, bottom right, the new building had taken shape.

First came demolition of buildings on the site, above left, and then nightlong pourings of concrete.

Come rain or shine, ice or heat, construction proceeded. Installation of copper siding and heavy glass windows brought the building into focus.

With machinery installed inside the building, long testing began, followed by adjustments and re-adjustments. Color reproduction and registration were checked on the press, right. Gripper conveyors, below, carried copies to Packaging and Distribution. Ink vats, below right, are color-coded. Bottom: The lobby.

As newsprint rolls and free-standing inserts enter the
Press Pavilion, they are monitored by employees, top left.
A conveyor moves the heavy loads, top right. For the new
presses' live runs, right, Star employees strip wrapping from
newsprint rolls. Afterward , the rolls are moved by conveyor
to the intermediate storage area between press lines, above.

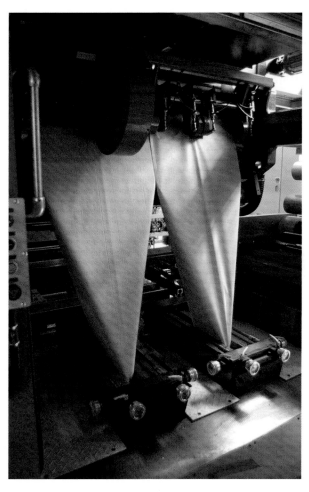

The press hall has four "quiet rooms" from which the presses are controlled, above. Complex arrangements of rollers and slicers perform the origami necessary to transform a long sheet of paper into a folded, multipage newspaper section, left.

Facing page: Modern press units require considerable vertical as well as horizontal space — one reason The Star needed a new building to contain its new presses.

Inside the Press Pavilion

2 Tanker trucks deliver five colors of ink — black, yellow, a greenish blue called cyan, a purplish red called magenta and a special bright-red ink used in some advertising. The ink is pumped through inlets at the receiving dock into color-coded vats inside the Press Pavilion.

Free-standing inserts, many produced by outside printers, are stored on racks and managed by the Automatic Storage and Retrieval System — ASRS.

3 When computer projections signal the need for more paper at the presses, the ASRS is alerted. Cranes remove the rolls from storage racks and place them on a conveyor. They move along at floor level to the preparation area near the presses. There, *Star* employees scan the attached bar codes to record the rolls' arrival and remove shipping wrappers. They also apply pasters. These are adhesive strips that will be used to connect the new rolls to nearly empty rolls already running on the press. After that, a conveyor moves each roll to an intermediate storage area between the press lines.

1 Paper arrives from mills in the United States and Canada. It's packaged in rolls - typically 48 inches wide, 50 inches in diameter and weighing about a ton - and shipped by rail to a warehouse in northeast Kansas City. Trucks haul it to the Press Pavilion. In the newspaper industry, this paper is called newsprint. At the receiving dock, newsprint rolls are moved to a conveyor, where their arrival is recorded electronically. From that point until they're called for at the press, they're managed by the computer-based Automatic Storage and Retrieval System. Automated cranes place them in storage racks in the northeast corner of the Press Pavilion.

Advertising insert machines

KBA Commander In-line presses

Newsprint and insert storage

PRESS HALL

Administration

Quiet room

Star trucks deliver cop throughout metro area

NORTH

4 In *The Star*'s headquarters building southwest of the Press Pavilion, staffers in the news division have been preparing news articles, photographs and images. The advertising division has prepared display and classified advertisements. All these elements are arranged electronically on digital versions of the newspaper page. Once the elements of a page are assembled, the digital file is sent by underground fiberoptic cable to the Press Pavilion's plateroom.

An electronic device called a raster image processor converts the digital file into a format that can be used to control an ultraviolet laser. The laser exposes the image of the page - all its type and images - onto a thin, flexible aluminum sheet called a plate. After exposure, each plate moves through a chemical bath that develops the image on the plate surface. Each plate is notched at the ends so it can be aligned precisely with other plates. Also, it's crimped for attachment to a press cylinder.

5 Pressmen carry the plates to the presses and attach them to plate cylinders.

A black-and-white page impression requires only one plate containing black ink. Each extra color on a page requires an extra plate. A four-color page requires four plates for a full page impression.

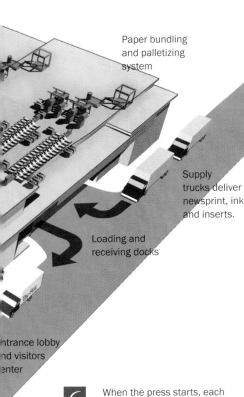

Paper bundling and palletizing system

Supply trucks deliver newsprint, ink and inserts.

Loading and receiving docks

ntrance lobby nd visitors enter

The Palletizer

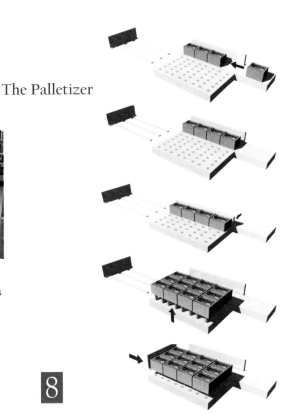

6 When the press starts, each plate cylinder begins to rotate. A watery mixture is sprayed on rollers. From the rollers, it's applied smoothly to the rotating plate cylinder. This watery mixture adheres to the parts of the plate where no image appears. To another set of rollers, ink is applied. The rollers transfer the ink to the same plate cylinder. Ink contains oils and, like any oil, ink won't mix with water. As it's applied, it is repelled from the non-image part of each plate by the watery mixture, but it adheres to the image part. From the plate cylinder, the inky image is transferred to a blanket cylinder, and from that cylinder to the paper streaming up through the press. Both sides of the paper are printed simultaneously.

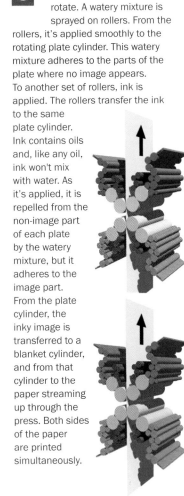

7 As paper empties off a roll and begins to wind its way through the press, it's called a web. Web presses like *The Star*'s are designed to print hundreds of thousands of copies speedily and efficiently. Racing through the press, the web passes over the inked blankets. Then the web follows a circuitous path through sets of rollers that turn it and fold it, again and again. Eventually, the streams of paper combine in the press to become sections. Each copy is cut and mechanically folded, finishing the conversion of what was a single stream of paper into recognizable copies of a newspaper.

As each printed and folded copy emerges from the press, it's picked up by a yellow gripper, one of thousands attached to long conveyor lines. The copies are carried overhead, out of the pressroom and into packaging and distribution in the south portion of the Press Pavilion.

8 In Packaging and Distribution, the freshly printed newspapers descend into bundle-stacking machines. These machines count out the number of copies specified for each bundle and drop them onto a platform.

Bundles are tied mechanically, and then travel along a line of rollers to the automatic palletizer. The palletizer pushes each bundle into a row until four are lined up. The machine pushes the row away and receives four more. Three rows, totaling 12 bundles, compose a layer. Long tines move under the layer, lift it and place it on a pallet. Atop each layer goes a cardboard sheet. Once the required number of layers is stacked, the pallet moves on rollers to an elevator that descends to the loading dock below.

Most days, *The Star* is printed in two or more parts. Parts printed early often are used to hold free-standing inserts. These parts are loaded into one or more of the long inserting machines in the Packaging and Distribution area. Inserts, meanwhile, are loaded by staff onto heads along the inserting machine. As an open jacket passes beneath each head, an insert drops into it.

From the loading dock, trucks deliver pallets of newspapers to one of *The Star*'s distribution centers throughout the metropolitan area, or to bundle drops farther away. Independent carriers pick up newspapers in their own vehicles and deliver them to subscribers' homes and to single-copy racks and boxes.

Packaging and distribution occupies a vast area in the
south half of the Press Pavilion. Employees prepare
free-standing inserts, top. Meanwhile, others move
more inserts into position, above. Gripper lines travel
many courses through the packaging area.

Facing page: The Press Pavilion from above,
completed.

Following page: Kansas City skyline view from atop
the presses.

Bibliography

Files of *The Kansas City Star, Kansas City Times, Kansas City Journal* and *Kansas City Post.*

Bell, William. "Historical Study of the Kansas City Star since the Death of William Rockhill Nelson, 1915-1949," University of Missouri thesis, August 1949.

"The First 100 Years," reprint in book form of special centennial sections of The Star published Sept. 14, 1980. Project editor was Michael Nelson, and the reporters were James J. Fisher, Phil A. Koury, Bleys W. Rose and others.

Garnett, Edward B. "My Life on The Star". Unpublished manuscript, ca 1960.

Larsen, Lawrence H., and Hulston, Nancy J. *Pendergast!* Columbia: University of Missouri Press, 1997.

McCorkle, William L. "Nelson's Star and Kansas City, 1880-1898". University of Texas dissertation, 1968.

Montgomery, Rick, and Kasper, Shirl. *Kansas City: An American Story.* Kansas City: Kansas City Star Books, 1999.

Reddig, William M. *Tom's Town: Kansas City and the Pendergast Legend,* :J.B. Lippincott Co., 1947.

Rogers, Charles Elkins. "William Rockhill Nelson: Independent Editor and Crusading Liberal." University of Minnesota thesis, 1948.

Stout, Ralph. *Nelson of "The Star"* Unpublished book in proof form, ca 1921

Wilson, William H. *The City Beautiful Movement.* Baltimore: The Johns Hopkins University Press, 1989.

Acknowledgments

You can't work at *The Kansas City Star* long before you run into William Rockhill Nelson. His full-figure portrait greets you on the way in the door, and other likenesses hang from walls in conference rooms and offices throughout the company. The most helpful employees annually win an award called The Full Nelson. If you've worked for the company three decades or more, as I and many others have, you've heard many people talk about how *The Star* used to be and how it ought to be, its traditions, its spirit and its myths. My first thanks, then, must go to all those who've gone before us current employees. They kept the facts, the legend and the culture alive, and kept the traditions before us.

Archival material is available in mass in *The Star*'s library, where Derek Donovan and his staff remain patient and understanding no matter how many questions I asked. But *The Star* doesn't have everything, and much resides with Mary Beveridge and her staff at the Kansas City Public Library's Missouri Valley Special Collections Department.

Production of a book is difficult, particularly one with lots of images, but this book was made much easier with the help of The Star's Jo Ann Groves. Mike Arnold and Dustin Dade pitched in, making fine reproductions from long-neglected negatives and even motion picture film.

Finally, thanks to Arthur S. Brisbane and his successor, Mac Tully, to Mark Zieman and to Sharon Lindenbaum for their support.

- Monroe Dodd

"When the news is gathered and prepared it must be gotten to the reader with the utmost swiftness. Newspaper presses are like race horses, capable of intense brief exertion and constantly in the pink of condition."

— "About the Kansas City Star Office," booklet produced by *The Star* in 1911.

Illustration credits

Photographs and other illustrations are from the news archives of *The Kansas City Star* except as noted here.

After the first reference, the Missouri Valley Special Collections Department of the Kansas City Public Library has been abbreviated MVSC/KCPL, and the Advertising Photo Department of *The Kansas City Star* has been abbreviated *Star* Ad Photo.

Dust jacket: Aaron Leimkuehler, Advertising Photo Department of *The Kansas City Star.*

ii-iii. Jean Dodd.
xii. MVSC/KCPL.
3. MVSC/KCPL.
8. Middle and bottom: MVSC/KCPL.
9. MVSC/KCPL.
11. MVSC/KCPL.
17. MVSC/KCPL.
24. MVSC/KCPL.
27. Lower right: MVSC/KCPL.
28. Upper left: Used by permission of the University of Missouri-Kansas City Libraries, Special Collections Department.
32. MVSC/KCPL.
43. MVSC/KCPL.
49. MVSC/KCPL.
58-59. Top: MVSC/KCPL.
62. Jack Wally Collection, Western Historical Manuscript Collection, University of Missouri-Kansas City. Photograph taken by Jack Wally.
63. Lower right: MVSC/KCPL.
71-72. Bottom center: Wilborn & Associates.
86. Bottom: MVSC/KCPL.
87. Top: MVSC/KCPL.
113. *Star* Ad Photo.
114. Jean Dodd
115. Top, Brandon Baker, *Star* Ad Photo; bottom left and right: Jean Dodd.
116-117. Top: Brandon Baker.
116. Lower left sequence: *Star* Ad Photo.
117. Middle left: *Star* Ad Photo; middle right and bottom: Brandon Baker.
118. Top left and right: Brandon Baker; bottom: *Star* Ad Photo.
119. Top and bottom right: Brandon Baker; bottom left: Landon Collis, *Star* Ad Photo.
120. Top, middle and bottom right: Brandon Baker; bottom left: Katherine Vescovo, *Star* Ad Photo.
121. Top, left and right, and bottom: Jean Dodd.
122. Jean Dodd.
123. Aaron Leimkuehler.
124-125. Diagrams: Gentry Mullin, *The Kansas City Star*. Photographs: Jean Dodd.
126. Jean Dodd.
127. Aaron Leimkuehler.
128-129: Jean Dodd.